Railways Around London

Compiled by John Glover
From the Alan A Jackson archive 1953 - 1973
at The Transport Treasury

The
· Transport ·
Treasury

Above: The Tilbury line was high in the list of electrification priorities which stemmed from the British Railways Modernisation Plan of 1955, that work being completed in 1962. Until then, the services between Fenchurch Street and Southend continued to be provided by steam traction, as seen here. On 16 February 1957, a down train headed by a Standard Class 4 2-6-4T approaches the platforms at Bromley. Those of the Underground are on the right. These locomotives always looked much more powerful than their Class 3 and Class 2 cousins, as indeed they were. This was due in part to the rounded side tanks, seen to advantage in this picture. In December 1957, 16 of these locomotives were allocated to the shed at Plaistow and a further 12 to Tilbury. The few remaining British Railways services ceased to call here and at other intermediate stations served by the District line, other than Barking and Upminster, after 1962. Bromley was renamed Bromley-by-Bow in 1967 to avoid confusion with Bromley North and Bromley South in the London Borough of that name. This preceded the transfer of station ownership from British Railways to London Transport, who were providing all the rail services, on 1 January 1969. Curiously, when the station's ticket office building, which had been renovated by British Rail was largely destroyed by fire in February 1970, it was British Rail who paid for its rebuilding. *Ref. AAJ 2693.*

© Images and design: The Transport Treasury 2021. Text John Glover

ISBN 978-1-913251-15-4

First Published in 2021 by Transport Treasury Publishing Ltd. 16 Highworth Close, High Wycombe, HP13 7PJ

www.ttpublishing.co.uk

Printed in the UK by Henry Ling Limited, at the Dorset Press, Dorchester. DT1 1HD.

Contents

Front cover: This is Shortlands, a London, Chatham & Dover Railway station, opened on 3 May 1858. The train is formed of 4-SUB unit No. 4304. This was from a batch of 26 suburban stock trains, built in 1925 as three car (3-SUB) sets, later given an additional trailer to make them up to four cars. They consisted of two seven compartment motor coaches, one nine compartment trailer and one ten compartment trailer, giving a total of 350 seats. These trains were built new for the Southern's expanding third rail electrification schemes, but were in many ways similar to earlier builds of converted steam stock. Another source was the trains built for the Brighton's ultimately unsuccessful overhead electrification. The S headcode with a bar above signifies a train from Sevenoaks and Orpington to Blackfriars. It is 12 July 1958. It is unclear as to whether the driver has stopped the train short, and the nearest passenger was waiting in vain for it to draw up a bit further, or whether the door was opened prematurely and the train is still moving. Main line operation here was still using steam traction, as the state of the canopies on the down platform bear witness. It is easy to forget, more than half a century after the end of steam on the national system, just how filthy it could make the stations and anything else in the vicinity. *Ref. AAJ 3549.*

Title page: Railway stations may have prominent city centre positions, or they may be hidden away down a side road. Fenchurch Street, seen here on 23 March 1963, is in the latter category and is actually located in Fenchurch Place. Does this affect their usage levels and hence their earning power for the train operator? Perhaps, but in this case the station is used by most as the city destination for commuters on the services from Southend and elsewhere on the London, Tilbury & Southend system, so this would be of only limited importance. It is the only London terminus without direct interchange to the Underground; Tower Hill is quite close by (as long as you leave by the central Coopers Row exit), Aldgate a little further, or Bank (for the Central line and the West End) is a long trudge. Constructed in 1853, the main concourse and trains are 39 steps above street level, though there are now escalators and lifts as well. The station has four platforms, the tracks of which then negotiate a comprehensive series of scissors crossovers. This allows the maximum number of what would otherwise be conflicting movements to take place simultaneously. The four track layout reduces to two tracks at Christian Street Junction (61 chains from the terminus). The rest of what was formerly a four track formation to Stepney East (now Limehouse) was commandeered for use by the Docklands Light Railway. This opened on 31 August 1987 with a terminus at Tower Gateway, near the 'country' end of the Fenchurch Street platforms. *Ref. AAJ 4822.*

Rear cover: The original Uxbridge Underground station was opened in 1904 but was closed in 1938 when London Transport decided that they wanted a larger building more nearly in the town centre. The result was the present structure, opened on 4 December 1938. The general approach to the design is reminiscent of Cockfosters as the north London terminus of the Piccadilly line which was opened five years earlier. There are though some dimensional differences; Cockfosters dealt with trains to tube loading gauge only; Uxbridge caters for both tube trains (Piccadilly) and sub surface trains (Metropolitan). This photograph was taken on 5 September 1959 and shows a pre-1938 stock train in the centre track which has a platform on each side. On the right is an F stock Metropolitan train, a class which was widely used on the Uxbridge line. Their last appearance here was still a few years away, on 15 March 1963. Passengers entered and left the paid area of the station through the traditional manned barrier, as seen on the left. Staff though were wanted, as the poster advertising gender specific vacancies for 'Stationmen' and 'Stationwomen' indicated. Note though that they are only 'required'; there is no hard sell on the merits of such a job, such as the human contact which it entailed. *Ref. AAJ 4203.*

Introduction

This book contains a profile of Alan A Jackson's photographic work related to railways in the London area, over the period 1953 to 1973. The arrangement is geographical, starting with the railways on the north bank of the Thames and working from the London terminals outwards. Coverage moves anti-clockwise round to the railways on **the** south bank. London Underground is pictured on a line by line basis, with the sub-surface lines first as indeed they were on the scene first, followed by the tube lines.

Alan Arthur Jackson left his North London grammar school in 1939 and joined the civil service. In World War II he served with the RAF in the Middle East, Italy and France. He returned to marry Beryl, a Queen Alexandra army nurse, in 1949. They had three daughters and eight grandchildren followed.

Resuming his civil service career, he spent much time in HM Treasury, retiring to Dorking, Surrey, in 1984. Jackson was a leading authority on the transport and social history of modern London and the author of several books on these subjects. Of particular note are *London's Termini* (2nd edn 1983), *London's Metropolitan Railway* (1986), his pioneering study *Semi-Detached London* (2nd edn 1991), *The Middle Classes 1900 -1950* (1991), *Rails Through the Clay, A History of London's Tube Railways* with Desmond Croome (2nd edn 1993), and *London's Local Railways* (2nd edn 1999).

He lectured and conducted seminars at the universities of London and of York and acted as a consultant for several television series on London's suburban and social history. He was a prolific photographer, who had the curious habit of leaving his holdall on the railway platform while retreating further to take a photograph, and including it in the resulting picture.

He was a Fellow of the Royal Society Arts and President of the Railway & Canal Historical Society 1988-90, followed by Vice President 2007 -09. He died on 21 February 2009, aged 86.

All the photography is the work of Alan Jackson, the text is that of the present author, John Glover.

My aim has been to provide a balanced portfolio of Jackson's work across the whole of the London area. Clearly, though, this is constrained by the material made available, and the emphasis is on the local railway and its infrastructure. But the subjects covered in this book have not been well recorded by others. What was commonplace tended to be ignored, but Jackson has done us all a service in making his work available.

Generally, imperial measurements are used as being the most appropriate for the period. Railway distance measurements in miles and chains, derived from the very early days, do not translate easily into metric equivalents. Signal sighting distances and similar are measured in yards, while the position of signals in an absolute sense is measured in metres. Distances on London Underground generally are metric.

On occasion, your compiler has felt the need to stray well beyond the London boundaries in his selection of subject matter. But even suburban services are likely to have their termini outside Greater London and locations such as Bishops Stortford, Rickmansworth, Bracknell and Horsted Keynes are, he hopes, within the range of what might be considered fair game.

He has sought the opinions of others where he has had doubts, but there is always scope for error in such a wide range of subject matter. He trusts that any problems that readers might detect will be minimal.

John Glover
Worcester Park
Surrey

2020

National Rail, Anglia

This is the street view of Barking station building, serving both British Railways and London Transport trains, on 24 August 1957. The station was opened by the London, Tilbury & Southend Railway in 1854, though Underground trains did not start calling here until 1902. Several of the features of the building seen here can still be observed at the next station nearer London, East Ham.

Much of Barking station was demolished and rebuilt by British Railways, starting in 1956; the new station was completed on 29 September 1961. This view was replaced with that of a huge glass fronted block, spanning the forecourt. This covered virtually the whole of the eight tracks and the platforms immediately below.

In the distance can be seen a trolleybus on route 691, Barking to Barkingside. Based at Ilford depot, this is one of the SA class of trolleybus, No 1729. Built in 1942 with a Leyland chassis and Metropolitan Cammell Carriage & Wagon bodywork, it was destined for Durban, South Africa. However, shipping of this and the other 41 similar vehicles was considered too risky, and they were put to work in London instead. Unfortunately, at 8ft 0in wide they did not comply with the then British requirements (7ft 6in was the maximum allowed) and they were also too heavy. But if needs be, regulations can be manipulated, and official dispensation was obtained.

This vehicle lasted in London Transport service until 1959. *Ref. AAJ 3161.*

Above: One of the main problems at Barking, seen here looking towards London on 11 March 1956, was the huge amount of conflict between trains crossing each other's paths on the level. This was exemplified by the central position in this picture of the Underground tracks, with those of British Railways on either side. The solution was the construction of a substantial flyover and dive-under system, which allowed trains to and from the Tottenham & Hampstead line to access the Tilbury lines without obstruction, and kept the Underground totally apart from all British Railways services in an operational sense. At the same time, passengers interchanging between the eastbound District line and the down Southend line were provided with cross platform interchange, and the same happened in the westbound direction. In this picture, the very adequate widths of the platforms may be noted, together with the substantial array of semaphore signals. The signal box is Barking West. To the left, Fowler 2-6-4T No. 42276 is taking water. *Ref. AAJ 2253.*

Opposite: The North London Railway built itself some long lasting 0-6-0 tank locomotives at their Bow Works. They were designed by J C Park, their locomotive superintendent, with the first being completed in 1879. They were designed for freight duties and were later classified as in the 2F category. On 5 May 1956, No. 58859 was rostered to take a Locomotive Club of Great Britain 'Poplar and Edgware' special from the company's London Broad Street terminus to Victoria Park and Poplar. It is seen here at Millwall Junction, where the line continued straight ahead to Poplar, or curved to the right for North Greenwich, with intermediate stations at South Dock and Millwall Docks. All regular passenger services had been discontinued as long ago as 1926, though the station still looked remarkably smart. Here, the passengers are spreading themselves liberally over the permanent way, with many hoping to obtain that 'different' photograph. At Poplar, haulage by No. 58859 was to give way to ex-Midland Railway 3F 0-6-0T No. 47484, which would take the train to Canonbury and a further change of engine to a Great Northern 0-6-2 tank No. 69506. *Ref. AAJ 2340.*

Opposite top: Liverpool Street station was long distinguished by its being in two parts. First on the scene was the western train shed, much of which is seen here, with the two long platforms, Nos 9, straight ahead and 10 to the left. Built but a decade later was the eastern train shed with platforms 11-18 to the left of this picture. The diesel Class 37 No. D6707 on an engineering train is in Platform 12. To the right are the platforms Nos 1 to 8 for North East London and beyond. But the whole was made difficult for passengers to use, due to the need to go round the far end of Nos 9 and 10 to reach the other half of the station on the level. There was also a high level walkway, but that doesn't suit everybody. The surface route also provided a way to and from the Underground's Metropolitan and Circle lines. This view of 23 May 1964 shows a Class 40 in Platform 9, probably with a train for Norwich. The first 10 of this 2,000hp class, Nos. D200-D209, were shared equally between the Great Eastern and Great Northern. To avoid too much one-upmanship, though, D200 was allocated to the Great Eastern, then D201 to the Great Northern, followed by D202-D205 to the Great Eastern and D206-D209 to the Great Northern. On the left of the Class 40 is the station pilot, Class 15 No. D8234, which was responsible for any shunting moves required. The platforms for the double sided tracks to the right were used primarily for the Cambridge and King's Lynn trains. *Ref. AAJ 5188.*

Opposite bottom; It was decidedly unfortunate that the junction for the East London Line from the Great Eastern main line was from the fast tracks, that it faced towards Liverpool Street, and that it was only 48 chains from the buffer stops. Those factors seriously limited its usefulness, particularly as the main line services intensified in frequency. Its use for freight was similarly fraught. Bishopsgate Junction, as it was named, is seen here from a Great Eastern train on the down fast line on 14 May 1966. The whole of the East London line was then extant and the Shoreditch terminating platform for the passenger services of London Transport, as it then was, is seen on the far side of the bridge arch. It will be noted that the fourth rail electrification was confined to that one platform and that's it. The other platform remained in situ, but there was no longer any means of access by passengers. This Shoreditch station was abandoned on 9 June 2006 in connection with the creation of the London Overground line which now runs north from the original Wapping station, over new construction to a Shoreditch High Street station, opened 27 April 2010. It then curves north to join the old North London line formation, which formerly served the Broad Street terminus, and continues to Hoxton, Haggerston, Dalston Junction, Canonbury and Highbury & Islington. This is a third rail installation, terminating at Highbury. *Ref. AAJ 5670.*

Above: On 22 March 1958 an eastbound Central line train from central London is seen arriving at Stratford on what is now Platform 6. From here, a cross-platform connection could be made to the down line Shenfield electrics (out of sight to the left). There was a similar arrangement in the reverse direction. The original pre-war plan included further connections to and from Fenchurch Street for workers in that part of the City, and the double track line connecting the two was wired for overhead electric operation. However, the planned service never materialised, and the link was used for stock transfer purposes only. The never used platform at Stratford on the down side, devoid of track, is in the foreground of this picture. This would have clearly needed more rolling stock and the train crew to go with it, while in the time taken for passenger interchange the original train might well have got to Liverpool Street. It also assumed that Fenchurch Street could cope operationally with the additional services. The benefits might have been rather more theoretical than real. Later, the Fenchurch Street link was singled over the intermediate section, with the other trackbed made available for use by the Docklands Light Railway. *Ref. AAJ 3286.*

The electrification of the line from Liverpool Street to Shenfield, at 1,500v dc overhead, was completed in 1949. A key feature seen here on 24 April 1955 was the new flyover at the London end of Ilford station. This lifted what became the electric line tracks over the two fast lines, positioning them on the south rather than the north side of the formation. This in turn enabled the very heavily used cross-platform connections to be made with the newly extended Central line of London Underground at Stratford. The nearest (third) track in the foreground is a connection from the up fast to the up electric lines, once they have passed over the flyover. A similar connection is available for down trains.

Here, an up train from Shenfield is formed of AM6 (later Class 306) three-car sliding door units with open interiors. It is seen beginning the ascent on to the Ilford flyover. The route, including the 1956 extension to Southend Victoria and its newer, more conventional stock, was converted to the new standard of ac traction in November 1960. This involved, separately, the rolling stock, the infrastructure and the power supplies. The whole line was converted to 6.25kV ac. Services between Shenfield and Chelmsford, which had also been electrified at 1,500v dc were de-electrified for a time and operated by a diesel unit shuttle. That would be electrified at 25kV ac which, 20 years later would replace all the 6.25kV ac sections. *Ref. AAJ 1912.*

The Great Eastern was renowned for the slickness of its North East London steam operated suburban services. Unwilling, or maybe unable, to finance the very real costs of electrification, they set out to see the very best they could do with steam.

This is Platform 1 at Liverpool Street on 5 May 1956, with an unidentified Class N7 0-6-2T at the stops. It is at the rear of the Quint-Art set (Quintuple-Articulated 5-car set) which it has brought in. Another locomotive is already attached to the front.

A similar formation may be seen in Platform 3, and in both cases the locomotive at the rear has access to a water column. In the peak, such sets were usually run in pairs. They had an enormous capacity; in their straight through compartments, six people could be sat on each side, with another six standing. That made 18, but if needs must, another two could just about get into each of the luggage racks, total 22.

For a very short while in 1875, Platforms 1 and 2 were connected to the Metropolitan Railway lines in the Baker Street direction. Quite what was to be gained by such a connection is obscure, but it did happen. This resulted in a bridge connection for passengers to Platform 1, while a gracefully curving section of the disused tunnel later housed a dining club for the British Railways staff. *Ref. AAJ 2332.*

Above: Services to Enfield and Chingford were entrusted to a fleet of 52 three-car non-gangwayed units built at York in 1960. This is unit No. 402, later No. 305 402 arriving on 14 May 1966 with a train on the down Suburban line at Bethnal Green. It was photographed from an unidentified train on the down Electric line. The Electric is thus named following the Shenfield electrification of 1949 when it was the only electric service at Liverpool Street. This was a 1,500v dc system, and the supports for the 6.25kv ac system where the Enfield train is travelling are noticeably less intrusive. The overhead wiring is also of less diameter, meaning that it is both lighter and less costly than that for the dc, and the dimensions of the supporting equipment can be reduced accordingly. Bethnal Green station now has two side platforms only, the island in the foreground having had its nearer platform removed, Trains that are to call here, and/or at Cambridge Heath and London Fields must use these lines, as there are no platforms on what are designated the fast lines before reaching Hackney Downs. *Ref. AAJ 5671.*

Opposite top: With steam operation of the North East London suburban services in its final throes, N7 0-6-2T No. 69647 is arriving at Hackney Downs with a Liverpool Street to Enfield Town train on 12 November 1960. All the signs of electrification are in place. All four tracks here are electrified; the two on the left are normally used by Chingford trains and also the main line and local services via the Lea Valley. This route remained un-electrified and a fleet of diesel units was purchased for local services. Main line operations continued with locomotive haulage as before. This was long before the Victoria line of London Underground was created, together with the interchange potential at Tottenham Hale, let alone services to Stansted Airport. The Lea Valley was mostly low lying land and had never attracted much in the way of house building. That was concentrated on the higher ground further west, to be served by the Enfield line. However, the lack of electrification denied the operators of an alternative route to Cheshunt should there be a problem on the route via Southbury. For that reason and also the increased possibilities of traffic gain on the Lea Valley, that too was electrified, with the work completed in 1969. *Ref. AAJ 4413.*

Opposite bottom: An Enfield Town to Liverpool Street train with Class N7 0-6-2T No. 69660 at its head, is coming to a stand at Bush Hill Park. While the locomotive crew are looking out down the platform, the Guard, if that is who it is in the first vehicle, seems to be in danger of nodding off. The train had only come three quarters of a mile! The destination board mounted on the bunker will be noted; this was common practice on the London suburban services on both the Great Eastern and Great Northern sections of the London & North Eastern Railway. If the correct board was not for any reason being carried, the custom was to turn whatever was available upside down, to signify that it did not apply on that journey. Well, it was customer friendliness of a sort! It is 13 September 1958 and services ran every 10 minutes during the peak, dropping to 15 or 20 minute intervals off peak. Work on the forthcoming electrification is yet to be seen in this view from the station footbridge. Gone will be the elderly articulated steam stock and steam traction itself, while the overhead masts and catenary will require the station canopies to be cut back to gain sufficient clearances. *Ref. AAJ 3689.*

This view, taken looking off the end of Enfield Town station platforms 1 and 2, shows no fewer than seven of James Holden's Class N7 0-6-2 tanks, most if not all of them in steam. The locomotive in front of the signal box is taking water from the water crane. The locomotive shed is on the right, out of the picture, and coal is being shovelled from the 21-ton mineral wagon into (presumably) the bunker of yet another locomotive of this class.

The overhead electrification equipment is in place as indeed it needed to be. This was Saturday 12 November 1960 and the steam services were to be replaced by electrics (but still in steam timings) two days later on Monday 14. The full electric services, in the new timings, commenced on Monday 21 November.

'At last', *Trains Illustrated* enthused 'with the long-desired help of electricity, and now in a form both swifter and vastly more comfortable for the passenger, the brilliant Great Eastern Railway experiment of 1920 (of providing the best possible steam service) has found its ultimate fulfilment'.

Unfortunately, the newly electrified services experienced many equipment failures on the trains themselves. This resulted in an emergency reduced service being introduced from 12 December, as too many trains had become unavailable. Steam operation was not restored, unlike in Glasgow where similar failures had occurred. Even so, the British Transport Commission was able to report that passenger receipts from these services in 1961 were more than 30% higher than in 1960. *Ref. AAJ 4417.*

The Great Eastern Chenford (<u>Ch</u>ingford, <u>En</u>field and Bishops Stort<u>ford</u>) electrification of 1960 resulted in Bishops Stortford, seen here, becoming the end of the 25kV system. This view of 12 September 1959, looking north from the footbridge, shows the station in the course of reconstruction. The two tracks to the left serving platforms 1 and 2 are the down and up main lines respectively. That on the right of the island platform (Platform 3), was originally used for trains to Dunmow and Braintree, the passenger services on which were withdrawn on 3 March 1952.

This track was connected to the up main line as shown here and resignalled to allow for reversible working in the platform. This enabled the terminating electric services from the reopened route from Liverpool Street via Southbury to use the end of the platform behind the camera, with connections to and from local destinations further north using the remainder. The other two tracks and platforms thus remained available for through traffic. Nowadays, all lines are reversibly signalled.

Also of note is the turntable, complete with an unidentified locomotive. There was an extensive goods yard here. Above the platform is what appears to be somewhat perilously secured lighting. It is presumed that this would later be attached to a concrete column.

Trains to Cambridge and King's Lynn were to continue to be diesel locomotive hauled until electrification was continued northwards. This was in conjunction with the electrification of the Great Northern route beyond Royston, which eventually reached King's Lynn. The principal trains, all electric units, were transferred to this route, while the Great Eastern services generally were terminated at Cambridge. They also had to accommodate additional services with the opening of the branch to Stansted Airport in 1991. *Ref. AAJ 4234.*

Opposite top: This is the north end of Bishops Stortford station, looking south on 12 September 1959. Electrification was clearly coming and as a starter the footbridge is being reconstructed. The semaphore signal giving access to platform 3 (left) seems a little uncertain as to whether it is displaying an 'on' or 'off' indication. That is potentially dangerous, but it is probable that the signalman is merely in the process of altering its position. The line into Platform 3 is on a curve, and the cant on the track (one rail higher than the other) may be observed. A steam locomotive is in the main down platform 1, but there is no further identification. Note the grounded van body on the left, with other detritus that tends to surround motive power locations. Electrification would bring a half hourly service to Bishops Stortford, via Southbury, upped to every 20 minutes in the peaks. There would also be a two hourly service to King's Lynn, with some additions to Cambridge only. The electrics with 10 intermediate stops managed to reach Stortford in 56 minutes from Liverpool Street; the non-stop diesel hauled King's Lynn services took 37 minutes. This was in 1964. *Ref. AAJ 4236.*

Opposite bottom: The wayside station of St Margarets (Herts) is on the Broxbourne to Hertford East branch of the Great Eastern. The station name is not to be confused with that of St Margarets (Greater London), though it is not unknown for passengers to end up at the wrong one. This is the Hertfordshire station on 19 September 1964. A good number of passengers are awaiting their train towards Liverpool Street, some of whom will have changed from the Buntingford branch diesel unit service in the bay platform behind them. There is also a smattering of passengers waiting for a service towards Hertford East. An unusual feature of this station is the signal box mounted on the down platform, making it very much part of the station. In the goods yard on the right, a mobile crane is attending to a line of goods wagons, which includes a high-sided open loaded with cable drums, a couple of Vanfits, a 16ton mineral and a BR Brake Van. *Ref. AAJ 5370.*

Above: The station for the town of Buntingford was situated at the end of a 13¾ mile branch line from St Margarets; there were no fewer than six intermediate stations. Journey times thus tended to be rather long, taking 26 minutes from end to end and calling at Mardock, Widford, Hadham, Standon, Braughing, and West Mill. That required a very quick turnround at both ends to enable an hourly service to be provided with one diesel unit. This could be helped by omitting Mardock, Widford and West Mill, which saved four minutes overall. Latterly, there were nine trains each way on Mondays to Fridays and 12 on Saturdays. The curious aspect was that on Mondays to Fridays no trains left St Margarets between the 08:58 and 15:33. On Saturdays there was in addition a 11:35, a 13:18 and a 14:20. Otherwise, the timetables were very similar. There was no Sunday service. This view is of the Buntingford terminus on 19 September 1964 with a general air of dereliction and a lack of any goods traffic. The line was shown in Dr Beeching's *Reshaping of British Railways* as a passenger service to be withdrawn, and this took place a few weeks following this photograph on 16 November 1964. *Ref. AAJ 5367.*

National Rail, Eastern

It would take a lot to lift the air of gloom from the Widened Lines part of Moorgate station, seen here on 30 January 1971. The area suffered considerably from aerial bombardment during World War II, requiring a major rebuilding exercise. One particular aspect of this was the straightening out of the curves of the two parallel railways between Barbican and Moorgate stations. This work was completed in 1965. That enabled the Barbican redevelopment to go ahead, with large sections of the railway subsequently covered in. At Moorgate, Platforms 1 & 2 are for the Metropolitan, Circle and Hammersmith & City lines, 3 & 4 for terminating Underground trains from the west, and 5 & 6 for Widened Lines trains. This Cravens diesel unit (later Class 105), seemingly only a 2-car unit, is stabled in the Great Northern's usual Platform 6. Midland services used Platform 5. The blind says Hatfield and the train carries an oil tail lamp. While there were thoughts that the whole of these platforms might be roofed over, this did not take account of the exhaust from diesel locomotives, then to be found here, or the diesel units that followed. Accordingly, vents were left to allow the fumes to escape. With the expanded Thameslink to become a reality, Farringdon platforms needed lengthening. This forced the issue of the Widened Lines closure to Barbican and Moorgate, which took place on 20 March 2009. With new connections, the tracks may yet have a future use for stabling London Underground stock. *Ref. AAJ 6668.*

Above: By no stretch of the imagination could King's Cross Metropolitan have been termed an attractive location. It is seen here on 2 July 1958, with a Class N2 0-6-2T approaching from Moorgate with a Great Northern line train for Hatfield. The destination display, on the chin as it were, certainly helped passengers to identify the train correctly. As can be seen, there are no creature comforts on the platforms. The Metropolitan line platforms, at one time parallel with these to the right, were moved to their present below ground location in 1941. This left the Widened Lines platforms (which were shared with the Midland) for British Railways services to make what they could of them. In the 1970s, the introduction of the Great Northern Suburban electrification from Moorgate via Highbury & Islington saw the end of such services here, while the residual Midland train service soldiered on. But then came the 'BedPan' (Bedford-St Pancras) overhead electrification, inaugurated eventually on 15 July 1983. The station was considerably cleaned up and was renamed King's Cross Midland City. That sufficed for a time, but there were greater ambitions for Thameslink. Such services started in May 1988 in a relatively modest way, but they did re-establish the closed rail link between Farringdon and Blackfriars. Another renaming took place, with the station becoming King's Cross Thameslink. The final phase, on 9 December 2007 saw this station closed and replaced by new platforms beneath London St Pancras International station. *Ref. AAJ 3507.*

Right: An unidentified Deltic in Rail Blue, 3,300hp from the English Electric Co, is being backed down at what was then Platform 8 at King's Cross on to a train for Newcastle. It is 23 October 1971. Note that the driver in what will become the front cab is being guided by hand signals from a second man in the nearer cab. Track curvature in particular can make it difficult for the driver to see adequately in such circumstances. The headcode on the locomotive refers to its last journey to London. This was a Class 1 train

(express passenger) with an E destination (the old Eastern Region) and 39 being the individual train. For its journey north, the E will become N, signifying a destination in the old North Eastern Region. Such designations are still used for train identification purposes in, for instance, signalling centres, but they no longer appear on the trains themselves. The train itself has a MkIId 2nd class coach leading, then a newly built vehicle from Derby. These were among the very first air-conditioned coaches on the British Rail network. In the background may be seen a stationary Class 31 propping up the southern end of Gasworks tunnel, and part of a Class 47. For those who well remember such scenes, it is perhaps worth a reminder of how long ago it was. The age of the many young people in this picture is such that they are now likely to be in at least their sixties. *Ref. AAJ 6862.*

This is one of the classic views of King's Cross, taken on 25 January 1969 from the footbridge which spanned the station. It shows the four main line platforms on the western side of the train shed. On the left in what was then Platform 7 is a Deltic locomotive, having arrived from Edinburgh with 1A35, the up *'Flying Scotsman'*, and a train of earlier non air-conditioned MkII vehicles. The train was marshalled with the First Class coaches at the London end, which became standard InterCity practice. Platform 6 is free, but trains of MkI coaches are in both Platforms 8 and 10. Trains need heating in winter and tell tale wisps of steam can be seen emerging. This was sourced from the locomotive's train heating boiler, that was introduced to compensate for that which used to be provided as a by-product of steam traction. It was always wise for passengers to sit as near the locomotive as practicable to ensure a warm journey. Electric heating was introduced only gradually. The curious platform numbering derived from the early days when the only platforms for passengers were those on the extreme right and (out of sight) on the extreme left. In between, there were only sidings. More platforms were added gradually, but at this stage their numbers were 1, 2, 4, 5, 6, 7, 8, 10 and stayed unchanged until renumbered as part of the extensive reconstruction and electrification in the 1980s. *Ref. AAJ 6210.*

King's Cross Platforms 14 and 15, left, were known as King's Cross Suburban and used accordingly. The heavily curved Platform 16, centre, was used by services originating from Moorgate, with the peak hour only services on the Widened Lines to King's Cross, and thence to various destinations. The steepness of the gradient was the undoing of the Cravens Class 105 diesel units. Built for the bucolic territory of the Midland & Great Northern across East Anglia but never used there as it was closed in 1959, they were employed instead on King's Cross inner suburban services. However, with a full rush hour load and limited power, they could not be relied upon to start on the steep gradient here. After some unfortunate incidents, they were banned from undertaking Moorgate peak workings; this resulted in the retention of locomotives and hauled suburban coaching stock. This continued until the route was closed in connection with the Great Northern suburban electrification scheme.

Given the height of no 14 and 15 platforms above the far end of No. 16, the gently sloping pedestrian route from the concourse offered very fast access for those who were in danger of missing their train from No 16.

Platform 17, to the right, was used to unload general stores for the station, and also for the unloading or loading as appropriate of restaurant car vehicles on their way to or from workshops. These would be placed in the restaurant car stores below the station. This scene was photographed on 1 May 1965.
Ref. AAJ 5438.

Above: Class A3 Gresley Pacific No. 60082 *Neil Gow* stands in Platform 4 at King's Cross on 27 August 1958. It has presumably brought an express service in, but its tender is still remarkably well filled with coal. Behind it is the well known King's Cross signal box, with its excellent views of the station area. On the right, Thomson Class L1 2-6-2T No. 67794 is performing duties of a station pilot nature or similar. Also in view is the York Road platform, which opened in its permanent form on 4 March 1879. This offered what amounted to a King's Cross station stop for passengers on trains which would proceed to King's Cross Metropolitan and stations to Moorgate. From York Road, it was a long walk to the front of the main line station in Euston Road, while the equivalent departure platform of Platform 16 on the main station, for trains from Moorgate, was nowhere near the Euston Road either. This rather untidy arrangement ceased with the abandonment by the Great Northern of Widened Lines services with electrification of the former Northern City line to Moorgate and its incorporation into British Rail's suburban services. *Ref. AAJ 3654.*

Opposite top: The tracks for the Northern Heights scheme for London Underground were to rise from Drayton Park and form a new route on the surface to the east of the existing Great Northern main line, with platforms, at Finsbury Park. This picture shows the missing bridge work, looking south over Stroud Green Road with the station on the right on 1 May 1965. None of this work ever came to fruition and Finsbury Park station, which would have seen some serious upgrading, was left undisturbed. Only in relatively recent times have much needed efforts been made to improve the passenger parts of the station and access to the various lines that serve it. The twin tracks to the north were then to rise and cross the East Coast tracks by bridge to meet the then existing formation, continuing to Stroud Green, Crouch End and (sandwiched between two tunnels) Highgate High Level station. Trains would then proceed to Park Junction and bear right to reach Alexandra Palace. Alternatively, at Park Junction they would reach the existing Highgate Underground depot and could carry on the additional mile to East Finchley. This section is used by Underground trains for depot access, but not for the carriage of passengers. *Ref. AAJ 5441.*

Opposite bottom: The Alexandra Palace trains called at Highgate, the station dating from 1867. This view, looking north west shows the station platforms neatly contained between the two sets of tunnels. Access to them was via steps down to the ticket hall for the Underground, with access/ egress available from there to both sides of the line. The Underground station opened on 19 January 1941 and paralleled what was then the LNER line to East Finchley. The Underground platforms are reached by escalators from the ticket hall. This view shows a train from Alexandra Palace to King's Cross on the last day of service, 3 June 1954, after which these platforms at Highgate would be closed permanently. They are still largely extant, albeit without track and extensively overgrown. Apart from the cable run supports, there is little sign of what was intended to be the Northern Heights electrification to Alexandra Palace, High Barnet and Edgware, plus the brand new extension to Bushey Heath. Such were the ambitions of this part of the 1935/40 New Works Programme of the London Passenger Transport Board. *Ref. AAJ 1583*

Above: The branch to Alexandra Palace had two intermediate stations, at Cranley Gardens and Muswell Hill. This view of Cranley Gardens, taken on 17 October 1964, a decade after closure, shows stripped platforms, an overgrown trackbed, and the bridge carrying Muswell Hill Road at the platform ends. An inherent problem of the branch was that on leaving the line to Edgware a little beyond Highgate, which itself was heading north west, it then turned sharply north east to reach its terminus. As a consequence, Alexandra Palace station was 6¾ miles from King's Cross, whereas Wood Green on the GN main line (later renamed Alexandra Palace) was only five miles distant. Given journey times of around 25 minutes to Alexandra Palace with a fares premium as well, and 15 minutes to Wood Green, the branch did not have a lot to offer. It might be added that Cranley Gardens station was (and is) on a more direct bus route from Highgate Underground station. *Ref. AAJ 5385.*

Opposite bottom: The branch from Highgate to Alexandra Palace had a very chequered history. Originally opened on 24 May 1873, it was closed for the first time following a fire which destroyed the main Palace building on 9 June of that same year. After that its fortunes varied with that of the Palace itself, and the railway was closed for various periods, then reopened, no less than eight times. Apart from the Palace and its attractions, there was little reason for the branch station's existence. The branch was included in the 1935/40 New Works Programme of London Transport, under which it was to become part of the Northern line running north from Finsbury Park on the then existing Great Northern route to Finchley and Edgware. But only limited work was completed before the outbreak of World War II and in the event was never resumed subsequently. It lingered on, with the final indignity of service suspension from 29 October 1951 to 7 January 1952, due to coal shortages. In short, it did not prosper, while the likelihood of electrification and the introduction of an Underground service disappeared altogether. The last trains of British Railways ran on Saturday 3 July 1954, with the official closure taking place the following Monday 5 July. This is an unusual view of the station taken on the last day from the footbridge leading out from the Palace. It shows the branch train with an N2 0-6-2T in charge of two non-corridor coaches, ready to leave. There were two tracks facing the island platform, but only that on the Palace side had a run-round loop. In the distance, between the trees, can be seen the station signal box. *Ref. AAJ 1577.*

Above: Of the eleven stations on the Hertford North branch, only Bowes Park, opened on 1 November 1880, has an island platform. It is seen here looking north from the front of a diesel unit on 11 July 1970. The whole line became part of the Great Northern Suburban electrification in 1976. Island platforms on double track lines are good in terms of economy in the numbers of platform staff needed (in past times, anyway), but a bridge or subway is an essential for passengers entering or leaving the station. Passengers nowadays are most unlikely to be allowed to cross tracks on the level. Is the ticket office to be on the platform, on the access bridge (as here), or do you consider having one each side? Where should ticket barriers, or gates (if any) be installed? Or none at all? Do you need the station to be accessed directly from both sides of the line, especially if there is a nearby road bridge? Operationally, the need for the tracks to be splayed out to accommodate the island platform between them (as on the down line here) affects the trackwork geometry and also the maximum permitted speeds of trains that are not scheduled to stop. The Hertford North branch is a regularly used diversion from the main line between Alexandra Palace and Langley Junction, Stevenage. Semaphore signalling is still evident, and that for the entry to Bounds Green Traction and Rolling Stock Maintenance Depot is evident. *Ref. AAJ 6541.*

In 1906, there were three major impediments to the track capacity of the London end of the Great Northern. These were the truncation of the Enfield Chase line at that station, the double track section over Welwyn viaduct, through Welwyn North station and the two succeeding tunnels, and between Hadley Wood and Potters Bar. The extension from Enfield Chase to Hertford North and Langley Junction, a little short of Stevenage, was opened in 1913. The Welwyn double track section remains the same today, but the Hadley Wood widening was undertaken in the late 1950s.

This involved the reconstruction of Hadley Wood and Potters Bar stations, and their expansion to four platforms, the duplicating (on the west, left hand side, two tracks to four) of Hadley Wood South tunnel (seen here), 384 yards, Hadley Wood North tunnel, 232 yards, and Potters Bar tunnel, 1,214 yards.

The work was carried out using tunnelling shields. The shield was moved forward by rams pushing against the previous concrete ring, the segments of the next ring were positioned, the lower ones first, while the soil was excavated and removed by conveyor belt. The cycle then recommenced with the rams first pushing back the new ring to interlink with the previous one.

Colour light signalling and track-circuiting were installed throughout, controlled from a new box at Potters Bar.

This view shows the southern end of the future 2½ mile work site and Hadley Wood South tunnel on 20 August 1956. Class 9F 2-10-0 No. 92039, then nearly brand new, has taken the up fast rather than the up slow line with a coal train. At the time the photograph was taken, the four tracking then ceased at Greenwood Signal Box (left). The signalman and the lever frame were the subject of a painting by Terence Cuneo, *On Early Shift*, with a Gresley A4 Pacific approaching.

Hadley Wood station can just be seen through the tunnel. Six years of work were completed on 20 May 1959. *Ref. AAJ 2609.*

National Rail, Midland

Broad Street station opened on 1 November 1865; at the height of its usefulness, there were nine platforms (eight within and one outside the train shed) in use, but this traffic gradually faded away. This is the scene on 22 February 1964. What was described unexcitingly as a London District Three-Car BR Set, built at Eastleigh in 1957 (later Class 501) stands in Platform 7. Its destination is unknown, but the passengers look as if they are awaiting another train to arrive and couple up. Over the far side, a two-car Cravens unit (later Class 105) may just be seen. Unusually, British Railways 'sausage' signs in (presumably) London Midland Region maroon are perched on top of advertising panels on the platforms.

Electric services on dc fourth rail started from Broad Street in 1916, eventually covering many London area lines, but not those to the Great Northern or Great Eastern systems.

Post war the system stabilised with the electric services running as before, supplemented only by the Great Northern services but reduced to rush hours only. The Great Northern services would cease altogether on Saturday 6 November 1976 with the suburban electrification to Moorgate.

The remaining electric services were progressively downgraded and facilities were taken out of use. A new diesel unit service was started on 14 May 1979 between Camden Road and what was then the freight only line to Stratford low level and North Woolwich. The end of Broad Street was not far away.
Ref. AAJ 5106.

The concourse of Broad Street station was at platform level rather than that of the street, far below. Rather confusingly, that was Liverpool Street, a name more associated with the establishment which was almost next door. The concourse is seen as it was on 5 December 1970. In this view the war memorial to the 65 North London Railwaymen who fell in the Great War can be seen. It was erected in 1921 and was described by Sir John Betjeman as being like a miniature Cenotaph. This part of the station was reasonably light and airy, but on this occasion with only a few passengers. Broad Street seemed to suffer from passengers turning up late, missing their train, then complaining that the train had left early. Rather than arguing, the Station Foreman responded by telephoning the speaking clock and broadcasting the dulcet tones giving the time over the station loudspeakers. In 1985, a new and very temporary outlying platform was created for Broad Street passengers and the station was demolished. This was to make way for the construction of the huge Broadgate Centre. The last train ran on Friday 27 June 1986, with formal

closure on 30 June 1986. Following closure, the war memorial was found a place in Richmond station car park, but was relocated to a site outside Hoxton station in May 2010. There was also the need to cater for those wanting the City from the Watford direction. The Graham Road curve was put in to enable trains from the North London line to reach Liverpool Street station. Seeing a Class 313 set there with the blind saying Watford Junction did take some getting used to. However, changing trains at Highbury & Islington for Moorgate was a good bit faster for most people. *Ref. AAJ 6660.*

Above: If Dalston Junction on 22 February 1964 looks decrepit, that is sadly how it was. In those days there were six tracks, all leading to Broad Street on the left. The two tracks on the far left, Platforms 1 and 2, and only just visible, were used by the electric services to Richmond and Watford Junction. Platforms 3 and 4 were for trains to and from the Great Northern via Canonbury and Finsbury Park, while the two unnumbered and effectively disused ones on the right were for services to Stratford. Bombing raids during World War II resulted in the ordinary passenger services being suspended and they were never reintroduced. After the Camden Road – North Woolwich service was introduced in 1979, intermediate stations were opened at Hackney Central and Hackney Wick (both 12 May 1980), Dalston Kingsland (16 May 1983), and Homerton (13 May 1985). The next stage was third rail electrification of this link, with the Class 501s replaced by Southern 2-EPB sets (Class 416/3) and later Class 313s. After that, there was no real role for Broad Street, or Dalston Junction. Both stations were closed formally on Monday 30 June 1986, the last train having run on the previous Friday. There was however to be a resurrection of Dalston Junction under the auspices of London Overground. Although Broad Street was demolished and completely obliterated by the construction of the Broadgate Centre, much of the viaduct northwards remained intact. So it came about that a new station was built on more or less the same site, below street level and with two through and two terminating platforms. The new station was opened fully on 23 May 2010. *Ref. AAJ 5110 .*

Opposite top: The entrance to Highbury & Islington station was reconstructed by British Rail for the coming of the Victoria line, which supplemented their own North London line and what in those days was London Underground's Northern City line. The new building had been opened on 7 April 1968, but it was supposedly only temporary. It is seen here on the day the first section of the Victoria line opened, between Walthamstow Central, Blackhorse Road, Tottenham Hale, Seven Sisters, Finsbury Park and Highbury & Islington, on 1 September 1968. The weather was not of the kindest, but was the result really as bad as it seems here? There is poster reference to the North London line and a small sign directs passengers to the Underground. Another poster informs passengers about the Finsbury Park - Drayton Park coach service. This was introduced in 1964 as a result of the Northern City line service between these points being withdrawn to allow the construction of the Victoria line and the re-use of those platforms at Finsbury Park. There is a poster giving times for first and last Victoria line trains and the standard Underground diagram. All in all, it didn't seem aimed at enticing the crowds. *Ref. AAJ 6137.*

Opposite bottom: Highbury & Islington at platform level was not beautiful. It is 2 October 1971. There were four tracks here on the North London lines, the southern two for passenger services, and the northern two (out of sight to the right) used principally for freight. These were later electrified at 25kV ac; to reduce costs much of that part of the railway was also singled. Meanwhile, the fourth rail dc electrification soldiered on for the local services. A three-car Class 501 unit, one of a batch of 57 built at Eastleigh for the London Midland Region dc lines in 1957 is approaching, with a Richmond to Broad Street train. The centre vehicles were all closed compartments; how else do you get 108 seats in a 57ft long nine compartment vehicle? Enclosed compartments were however going out of fashion; one of them carried the green 'Ladies Only' transfer, probably one of the last so to do. They were later converted to open type seating. The driving end vehicles, one a motor, one a trailer, were built with the open design. The station facilities at platform level at Highbury & Islington were of a basic utility design, perhaps reflecting damage suffered during the 1939-45 war. *Ref. AAJ 6854.*

This page: Croxley Green was at the far end of a line from Watford Junction and Watford High Street, with an intermediate branch station at Watford West. A second short lived station was the private and match days only Watford Stadium, from 1982 to approximately 1991. This view is taken from the cab of a train about to depart from the Croxley Green terminus. The provision of the fourth rail, then in use on the London Midland Region London area dc services such as this, the existence of a disused run round loop and the timber platform construction may be noted. It is 15 September 1962. Then the service was being operated by the Class 501s. These were essentially Southern designed three car slam door EMUs; they differed from the standard Eastleigh production in that they had three bars on all the droplight windows due to tight clearances, were 57ft long vehicles rather than 64ft and, horror of horrors, they actually had a destination blind. What is more, the blinds were used! Croxley Green station was not particularly close to anything much, and by June 1993 the service had shrunk to only one train in each direction Mondays to Fridays only. Hertfordshire County Council wanted to drive a new dual carriageway road through the railway embankment without providing a replacement bridge. The result was that the last trains of the very truncated service ran on 22 March 1996. A bus replacement was provided; latterly this became a taxi on demand, before disappearing altogether. Formal closure of the branch took place on 29 September 2003. For a time, it was thought that a part replacement rail service might be provided by extending the Metropolitan line of London Underground from Croxley over some of the old formation to Watford High Street and Watford Junction, with two new stations en route. However, insufficient funding has been forthcoming. *Ref. AAJ 4738.*

Above: R W Urie was the Chief Mechanical Engineer of the London & South Western Railway who was responsible for the design of the huge G16 4-8-0 tanks for the working of Feltham hump yard. There were four in the class and No. 30495, seen here, seems to have escaped the yard when on 27 June 1957 it was photographed just short of the regional boundary between the London Midland and Southern Regions. It is on the down Kew line, south of South Acton station and junction. The locomotive is hauling a mixed freight, traffic long since lost to the railway, almost certainly bound for Feltham. The electrified line diverging to the right is that of the North London to Gunnersbury and Richmond, while on the left the higher level track of the London Underground branch from Acton Town can be seen. Out of sight in the foreground is Bollo Lane, which had (and still has) the unenviable distinction of having two very closely spaced level crossings, one for each of the two branches. *Ref. AAJ 3060.*

Opposite top: The magnificent roof of St Pancras station, designed by W H Barlow, is seen here from beyond the platform ends on 27 January 1968. The seven platforms are numbered from No. 1 on the far right to No. 7 on the left. After the turbulent time which followed when the station's future was seriously at risk, and the ultimately abortive plan to create an additional low level station for Channel Tunnel traffic, salvation was found. The suburban services were diverted away from the main station, with new underground platforms en route to Moorgate, while the main station platforms were extended way beyond the end of the roof. Numbers 1-4 were dedicated to East Midlands services, Nos. 5 to 10 for international Eurostars, and Nos. 11 to 13, outside the overall roof, for South Eastern services. Here, Modernisation Plan 'Peak' diesel locomotive No. D151, later No. 46014 (2,500hp with Sulzer engine and Brush electric transmission, all 136 tons of it) was shortly to depart from Platform 5 with the 14:50 to Nottingham Midland. It will be calling intermediately at Kettering, Leicester London Road and Loughborough Midland, arriving at Nottingham Midland at 17:04. That is an overall timing of 2hr 24mins, at an unexciting average speed of 51.5mph for the 123½ miles. Today, that journey with the same number of stops will take 1hr 40mins, at an average 71.4mph. Such is half a century of progress, and still with diesel traction. *Ref. AAJ 6022.*

Opposite bottom: Should parcels be carried by passenger train, or have their own dedicated services? Here at St Pancras on 19 August 1962 can be seen Motor Parcels Van No. M55989 with a motley collection of half a dozen vans behind it. It is standing in Platform 1, displaying an initial 3 in the headcode panel. This signifies that it is to form an 'Express Parcels Train composed of vehicles permitted to run at 90 mph, or over'. Examination of the vans and given the number of them, that seems a little optimistic. Signalling bell codes for such trains was a 1-3-1. (One beat on the bell, pause, three beats, pause, one beat.) These units were built in modest numbers by Gloucester Railway Carriage & Wagon Ltd as with this one in 1960. It was part of a run of 10 single units (with gangways for the Western Region units, without for the London Midland). These were later Class 128. Cravens Ltd of Sheffield also turned out three broadly similar Class 129 vehicles but on the shorter 57ft underframe. Rebuilding of other passenger diesel units to make them suitable generally for the carriage of parcels also took place. A St Pancras -Bedford diesel unit of Class 127 may be seen in Platform 3. These units had hydraulic transmission. *Ref. AAJ 4723.*

Opposite: It was coal traffic which really made the money for the Midland Railway, based in Derby, but beer traffic from the Burton-on-Trent breweries was also important. London, with its huge population was an obvious market, and rail an obvious means of transporting the barrels. Sufficient thought went into the design of the St Pancras terminal building (completed 1868) so that the girders and support columns in the undercroft were laid out in such a way so as to store the maximum number of barrels possible. In other words, the design reflected the finer point of a Burton beer warehouse. So far, so good, but how were wagon loads of barrels to be got from the track to the vaults? Beer barrels are heavy items, which won't respond well to be being dropped. The answer was this hydraulic wagon lift, located beyond the ends of what was then Platforms 4 and 5. Once the wagons had been lowered into the vaults, they were moved around using capstans and ropes over a network of tracks and wagon turntables. None of this was ground breaking technology, but the application was more than a little unusual. This view was taken on 27 January 1968, by which time the feature had fallen into disuse. Today, much of that basement is a public area, filled with shops as well as the ticket office and secure areas for departing and arriving Eurostar passengers. *Ref. AAJ 6023.*

Above: This view is of Silkstream Junction, on the Midland main line north of Hendon, taken on 23 March 1957 and looking north. On the up slow line is No. 42178 a Fairburn 2-6-4T built in 1945 with a local train of seven coaches bound for St Pancras. The Midland is four tracked, with the two fast lines on the left and the two slow lines on the right. Here there are six lines, the extra two being the up and down Hendon. These leave the slow lines at Silkstream Junction, where the standard pattern Midland signal box of that name can just be seen, pass over the main lines and form a six line formation by the time Hendon station area is reached. Their principal purpose was to enable Midland goods trains to reach Cricklewood sidings and, importantly, the Dudding Hill line which would take them across London to Acton Wells Junction with the North London line, then on to Feltham yard. It may be noted that despite the complications of the layout, there are only two turnouts in view; the fast lines are not involved. There is however a grade connection between them and the Hendon lines in the station area. As can be seen, the whole complex took up a very considerable amount of land. There are many telegraph poles, now a superseded item of railway equipment. Note too the Distant signal on the up Hendon line, with alternate sections of its post painted in black and white to draw the attention of train crews. For the benefit of the curious, the Silk Stream is a three mile long tributary of the River Brent, in the London Borough of Barnet. *Ref. AAJ 2766.*

Above: This view of the middle number platforms at Euston, Nos. 7 to10, on 2 May 1963, and the destruction all around, shows the extent of the reconstruction work then being undertaken. It also demonstrates just how much the buildings in the centre section have limited the length of platforms achievable. There were other limitations too, notably the road overbridges beyond the north ends of the platforms. These severely constrained the track layouts. The demolition of the Great Hall and the Doric Arch (the latter now only the name of a public house in the bus station area) was regrettable, but their removal was instrumental in producing a station that held together as a whole. Expansion of the original Euston, with the substantial buildings in the middle projected towards the station throat, never seemed to match any overall design objective. The 630v dc electric lines from Watford Junction used the platforms in the centre of the station. Following earlier ideas that they should terminate in a loop under the main line station (hard luck London Underground), wiser views prevailed and platforms were set aside for them. The fourth (now third) rail system can be seen in this view; today it uses platforms 9 and 10, each accommodating 10 cars. *Ref. AAJ 4840.*

Opposite: Main line stations need to offer means of passengers accessing them, and for enabling them to get away after completing their rail journeys. This view is of the cab rank at Euston on 2 May 1963. It filled up the space between platforms 2 and 3. There are around 30 black cabs here, awaiting custom; this may seem a lot, but bearing in mind that a main line train may carry around 500 passengers, cabs may well be needed in short order. In the distance on the left can be seen Euston House, the then Headquarters of the London Midland Region and later the British Railways Board. The reconstruction of the main line station required major work on London Underground, including the very unsatisfactory interchange between the Charing Cross and Bank branches of the Northern line. Work was also undertaken on the ticket hall and the escalators leading to it from the main Euston concourse. The Victoria line would not open here until 1968, while the lengthy walk to and from Euston Square for the Metropolitan and Circle lines remained untouched, as it still does. With electrification Euston was to become much busier, the advent of HS2 will add further to the passenger flows. One possibility for dealing with this is the long talked about construction of Crossrail 2, though that shows little sign of moving out of the future aspirations slot. Meanwhile, Euston station still provides for taxis. *Ref. AAJ 4835.*

Opposite top: Platforms 1 & 2 are quite clearly not in use, as this view of Euston of 30 April 1964 shows. Some of the track is missing, but a flat wagon laden with a variety of debris is standing in Platform 1. This is on the extreme east side of the station, with St Mary's church in Eversholt Street in the background. This photograph shows the extent of the curvature of the formation as it fanned out towards the buffer stops. These (and

Platform 3) were the arrival platforms; broadly speaking those on the other side of the central part of the station were used for departures. Such a separation reflected the one time commonplace method of removing the coaches of arrived trains to the carriage sidings for cleaning, before bringing them back to a departure platform. Local services with shorter trains occupied the middle platforms; they were merely reversed and underwent an engine change if they were hauled. In this picture, roof demolition is going ahead, to produce what would in essence be a barren wasteland before reconstruction could begin properly. The work was started on the east side of the station, seen here, and moved west as time progressed. *Ref. AAJ 5176.*

Opposite bottom: The sadly underpowered Class 40s were the mainstay of the West Coast Main Line in the electrification years. Here, an unidentified member of the class sits in Euston's Platform 3 having arrived with an up train on 30 April 1964, possibly the 07:40 from Glasgow Central. At this stage, passengers had rudimentary protection from the elements with the temporary shelter. Some barrowloads, probably newspapers, may be seen. The tarmac area is providing a temporary concourse of sorts, but passengers had to make the best use they could of the facilities made available to them. The principal planned diversions were the Manchester Piccadilly traffic to St Pancras (from Manchester Central running via Millers Dale in the Peak District) and from Wolverhampton High Level and Birmingham New Street to Paddington or Marylebone (from Wolverhampton Low Level and Birmingham Snow Hill via Banbury). Premium trains with supplements were the Midland Pullman (Manchester and First Class only) and the Birmingham Pullman. Euston had to remain in operable condition whenever possible. Those from Rugby could use the Great Central line to reach London and Marylebone was available as a terminus from other lines. There was not much in the way of real alternatives for most other towns served by the West Coast line. *Ref. AAJ 5177.*

Above: This view of Euston as seen from the country end of Platform 3 shows the situation as it was on 30 April 1964. It was the intention that no fewer than 11 platforms would be available for use at any one time. Their identities would vary as the work sites moved, meaning that the signalling and interlocking systems would have to be adjusted each time.   In 1837, the original London & Birmingham Railway station had two platforms. One was for arrivals, the other for departures, with the tracks in between used for carriage storage. That was for only three trains a day, each way. The line was completed with through trains to Birmingham on 17 September 1838, with a journey time for the 112 miles of 5¼ hours, an average speed of 21mph. Traffic grew quickly and the station was expanded, both in the 1840s and the 1870s. Growth was not only passengers, but also parcels traffic. By the 1890s, there were 15 platforms, 14 for passengers and one for parcels, a far cry from the modest beginnings. In the 1960s, a total of 18 platforms were built, 15 for passengers three for parcels. Phase I also included the construction of two bays, a parcels deck, signal box, staff buildings and workshops. This was completed in 1966. Phase II focussed on the passengers, with a spacious open concourse, ramped platform access and a travel centre. Taxi and car park facilities were beneath the main concourse building, away from the passenger circulating areas. *Ref. AAJ 5181.*

On 31 August 1968, 25kV ac electric locomotive No. E3080, having brought train 1A31 into Platform 1 at Euston and been detached, waits to depart light engine. In these days, with locomotive haulage a comparative rarity for passenger services, it is easy to forget quite how many additional movements were associated with detaching and reattaching locomotives. This takes time, as well as gobbling up track capacity. E3080 was one of 40 members of what would later become Class 85 and in this case numbered 85025. They were built by British Railways in their own workshops. The Class 85s were one of five types of broadly similar locomotives, the others becoming Classes 81 to 84. All had a Bo-Bo wheel arrangement, all delivering about 3,000hp, all weighing 80 tons or so, and all with 100mph capabilities. By such means, the government hoped to give several potential manufacturers the chance to win orders. Delivered in 1960 or thereabouts, inevitably, some turned out to be more satisfactory than others. The end prize turned out to be a modest order for 100 Class 86 locomotives, built by British Railways and Vulcan Foundry and introduced in 1965. A separate order concerned the Class 87s; these 36 locomotives were 5,000hp machines, appearing from 1973. Exported examples of these later types survive in both Bulgaria and Hungary. *Ref. AAJ 6131.*

The reconstruction of Euston was a major undertaking in all senses, but so too was the electrification of what became known as the EBML lines (Euston, Birmingham, Manchester, Liverpool). This is the scene looking north from Bletchley station on 27 June 1964. The main lines are to the left. Below the photographer are the present platforms Nos. 5 and 6. These are used for trains to and from Bedford and as can be seen the tracks veer sharply to the right on leaving the station area.

Electrification gantries abound, but the adding of catenary is still some way off. Signalling is still by semaphores, which look decidedly out of place amongst all the modernisation work. At that time, the crossings then sited south of the station enabled the Oxford-Bletchley-Bedford-Cambridge services to cross the main lines on the flat and continue without reversing in whichever direction they were travelling. Bletchley flyover had been built, but it was intended for freight use and disregarded passenger services.

The flat crossing was removed and will not be reinstated, which leaves the East West Rail group with a bit of a problem, of how both Bletchley and the station of Milton Keynes Central (opened 14 May 1982) can be served, economically and effectively. *Ref. AAJ 5273.*

Opposite top: Marylebone station was opened on 15 March 1899. This external view of the grand terminal building was taken on 26 August 1967. For the Manchester, Sheffield & Lincolnshire Railway, their London extension never really fulfilled its promise. Dubbed 'the last main line into London', it was an additional facility to those provided by the other railway companies. Towns such as Brackley and Lutterworth gained services that would never have otherwise been available, but Rugby, Leicester, Nottingham and Sheffield were already well provided for. Changing the company's name to Great Central had, one suspects, little effect. This view looks east along the station frontage. The signs for 'Buffet and Bar' are now in corporate lettering, while road vehicles are directed by the sign showing the way in and they are entreated to drive slowly. The covered pedestrian way leads from the station to the hotel, built as such but which later became the headquarters of the British Transport Commission and later the British Railways Board. From 1993 it once again became a hotel. The railway serving Marylebone was much truncated in the 1960s, to the extent that by 1969 passenger services ran no further than Aylesbury on the former main line and Banbury on the route via High Wycombe. The result was a concerted effort by railway conversion interests to close the railway and tarmac it over. British Rail even went as far as posting a formal closure notice which would have seen the cessation of all their services south of Amersham and on the line from Northolt Junction to Marylebone. London Underground's Metropolitan line services from Amersham to Baker Street would continue. But the tide changed in the railway's favour, and in a statement of 30 April 1986 the Board 'decided not to proceed' with the proposal. Since then, what are now Chiltern Railways services seem to have gone from strength to strength. *Ref. AAJ 5991.*

Opposite bottom: The Golden Jubilee of the Institution of Locomotive Engineers was celebrated with an exhibition in Marylebone Goods Yard on 12-14 May 1961. This photograph in seasonally warm weather shows London Midland Region ac electric locomotive No. E3059 (later No. 85 004), Southern 3rd rail dc locomotive No. E5004 (later No. 71 004), a London Transport A60 Metropolitan line Driving Motor, and a 1959 stock Piccadilly line vehicle. What might appear to be a gibbet hanging over the track is in fact a loading gauge, reflecting the location's normal Goods Yard status. Elsewhere could be found steam locomotives, the 4-4-0 Midland Compound No. 1000, BR's last steam locomotive to be built (only the previous year) 2-10-0 No. 92220 *Evening Star*, BR's one and only 8P 4-6-2 *Duke of Gloucester* No. 71000, and No. 60022 4-6-2 *Mallard*, holder of the world speed record for steam traction. Modern traction featured English Electric's Gas Turbine 4-6-0 No. GT3, a brand new Deltic No. D9003 (later No. 55 003 *Meld*), Hymek No. D7000 (later Class 35), Warship No. D867 *Zenith* (later Class 42), and Type 1 No. D8400 (later Class 16). Visitor numbers were reported to be well in excess of expectations and, as *Trains Illustrated* reported, a little peevishly, nobody even tipped off an ice cream seller to patrol the scene. *Ref. AAJ 4482.*

Above: West Ruislip has been the final destination of the north west branch of the Underground's Central line since services commenced on 21 November 1948, where the Underground runs parallel with the Great Central/ Great Western Joint line for some distance. West Ruislip though was not always seen as the terminus. A further 2¾ mile extension of the Central line beyond the Greater London boundary to Denham, Buckinghamshire, was under serious consideration, but was not pursued. This was lightly populated territory and has remained so; Green Belt considerations were and remain relevant here. As can be seen in this picture looking south on 6 June 1959, the Joint line at this point had two through tracks, with platforms only on the two loops. The Underground station, beyond, is more or less separate, and consists of a single island platform, as do the other six Central line stations on this side of North Acton. Ruislip depot is just out of the picture, to the left. While the Underground offers a frequent service, Chiltern Railways trains call only hourly. *Ref. AAJ 3986.*

National Rail, Western

Above: Paddington sees No. D1065 *Western Consort* getting ready to leave with the 13:30 to Penzance on 28 April 1973. The train is made up of MkII vehicles, but not yet the air-conditioned variety. This fleet of 74 diesel hydraulics, Class 52, were the last of the truly main line types of locomotives thus powered, so favoured by the Western Region of British Railways. Introduced in 1961, their performance was good, but the Maybach engines were described officially as 'expensive to maintain and little improved despite various modifications'. Their availability at around 60% was depressingly low. The locomotives were built at either Swindon or Crewe, No. D1065 being a Crewe machine. Withdrawals were under way from the early 1970s and were completed in 1977. As may be seen, the 'country' ends of Paddington platforms, and especially the low numbers such as No. 2 where this train is standing, suffer from quite severe curvature. This can pose problems in the stepping distances into and out of coaching stock. The longer the vehicle, the worse the problem becomes. The locomotive is under the Bishops Bridge Road bridge with the original 1838 terminus constructed wholly on the nearside of this road, a distance to the north (left in this picture). This site was more or less straight ahead at the end of the main line; it was the rebuilding on the present site, completed in 1854, which created the difficulty. This realignment put the platforms parallel to Eastbourne Terrace. *Ref. AAJ 7087.*

Opposite top: It is 10:10 at Paddington on the morning of 26 September 1971 and there are already plenty of passengers joining the train at Platform 2. It will leave for Penzance at 10:30. In this view, taken from the footbridge and looking towards the buffers, the volume of parcels traffic is noticeable. There are a number of well filled BRUTE trolleys (British Railways Universal Trolley Equipment). When behind a tractor unit they formed an impassable barrier for those trying to cross their path, while the noise when in motion seemed likely to contravene Health and Safety regulations. Royal Mail mailbags seem to form a large part of the total, a traffic which has largely disappeared from the railway. One of the trolleys is chalked NCL, standing for National Carriers Ltd. This is a reminder of the period that British Rail was being divested of activities such as the Sundries Division and its Road Motor fleet. These were transferred to the National Freight Corporation in 1969. Will all those parcels fit into the van of the Brake 2nd which has its doors open? Another vehicle of indeterminate type is next to it and may take some of the load. Other traffic may be for a following train. Watching the photographer is a group of four ladies, with just the slightest air of resignation. Might they be family members waiting for the photographer? *Ref. AAJ 6853.*

Bottom: Southall was an interesting place from which to observe the passing railway traffic. From the footbridge at the eastern end of the station platforms, Great Western 4-6-0 No. 5922 *Caxton Hall* is seen passing on the fast lines on 6 June 1959 with a down express of 10 coaches. In the background is the extensive Southall locomotive shed (81C), part of which now forms the Southall Railway Centre. To the right and curving away can be seen the now single track branch to Brentford and Brentford Dock. Also to be seen and parked is a Great Western razor-edge railcar. This is painted in crimson and cream livery. Later, they would be turned out in multiple unit green. The pair of relief lines nearer the camera (slow lines was not a description allowed on the Great Western) are beginning to separate from the fast lines, to allow an island platform to be placed here. *Ref. AAJ 3977.*

Top: The Brentford Dock branch made a trailing connection with the fast tracks of the Great Western main line at Southall. It was opened to the docks for goods traffic on 18 July 1859 and for passengers to a Brentford Town station on 1 May 1860. Its principal purpose was to allow the GWR access to the Thames and also the Grand Union canal, where the two waterways met. This allowed goods to be transhipped easily to barges. The new facility gave the company access to the London Docks, on a route available for broad gauge trains. Brentford Docks covered a large area, incorporating two miles of track, six warehouses and twenty cranes. But decline set in as road transport grew more competitive, and the docks were closed to shipping in 1964. The land was bought by the then Greater London Council and redeveloped for housing and a marina. The area is described as 'rich in history, nature and community'. The modest rail passenger service ceased, on 4 January 1942. An intermediate Trumpers Crossing Halt was opened in 1904, but lasted only until 1926. This picture of 9 March 1968 shows the truncated branch where the railway crossed the Great West Road (A4). The rest remained in being, serving the industries that were left. In 1976 the Greater London Council entered into an agreement to create a Waste Transfer Station on the branch, which created rail traffic of several trains a week. *Ref. AAJ 6033.*

Opposite bottom: The 6¼ mile Great Western branch from West Drayton & Yiewsley to Staines West was one that did not survive. It is seen here at Colnbrook station, which was also a passing place on this single track line on 25 September 1956. The locomotive is a Great Western 14xx 0-4-2T No. 1436 with an auto working. From the West Drayton end, the intermediate stations were Colnbrook (3 miles), Poyle Estate Halt (3¼ miles), Poyle for Stanwell Moor (3¾ miles), and Yeoveney (5¼ miles). Trains terminated at Staines West (6¼ miles). A journey time of about 18 minutes meant that a half hourly service using one train was not practicable, and a second train, possibly one of the Great Western diesel railcars, would be introduced at peak times. Poyle Estate Halt and Yeoveney were usually indicated as request stops. Where this was the case, the Western Region timetable issued strict instructions: 'Calls to set down and pick up passengers. Those wishing to alight must inform the Guard at West Drayton or Staines West, and passengers desiring to join should give the necessary hand signal to the driver. Trains depart Poyle Estate Halt 2 minutes after leaving Colnbrook for Poyle. Trains depart from Yeoveney 2 minutes after leaving Poyle or Staines West.' The service was listed to be withdrawn in the 1963 Reshaping Report and the last trains ran on 28 March 1965 after a branch life of roundly 80 years. *Ref. AAJ 2623.*

Above: There are two stations in Windsor & Eton, the South Western one with the suffix Riverside, and the Great Western one called Central. This is the grand entrance to Windsor & Eton Central on 22 January 1967, complete with the Great Western Railway Coat of Arms above the arch. Or maybe it is not quite so grand, as the clock has lost its hands. The station was opened on 8 October 1849, less than two months before that of the South Western's Riverside. The entrance was rebuilt by the Great Western Railway to mark Queen Victoria's Diamond Jubilee in 1897. Despite occupying a prime location opposite Windsor Castle, the station has not prospered; its extensive facilities seeing progressively less railway use. Platforms 3 and 4 were closed in 1968, followed by No. 2 in the following year. The exhibition *Royalty & Empire*, joint with Madame Tussauds, took up a major part of the vacated space and ran for a decade from 1982. Since then, it has become the Windsor Royal Shopping Centre. There have been abortive plans to link the two railways in Windsor. For the record, in 2018/19 the number of passengers using the stations in the course of the year (entries and exits combined) were 2.02m for Central, and 1.55m for Riverside. The recorded volume of interchange between them (they are not far apart) was very low. *Ref. AAJ 5855.*

Above: This is Windsor & Eton Central station as it was on 22 January 1967. It is at the end of the 2¾ miles long branch from Slough and there are no intermediate stations. The last mile or so is above ground level, mostly on a series of arches. This includes a bridge across the River Thames. The Windsor branch is at a disadvantage as its junction with the main line at Slough is from the fast lines. There is a bay platform here (No. 1), suitable for a one train shuttle service, but that means passengers on other Slough local services have to cross the footbridge to access it. Perhaps that is of little impact, although the not inconsiderable tourist traffic might feel otherwise. It does however mean that through trains to Windsor & Eton Central are not really a good idea from the operational point of view. That being so, a capacious multiple platform station at the Windsor terminus is not really needed. Such was the conclusion of British Rail which, faced with a proposal to create a major exhibition (now closed) in the station environs, decided that the branch would have to be content with the use of one platform only. That turned out to be the far Platform 1 in this picture. It can accommodate a six-car train. An extensive goods yard closed in 1964. *Ref. AAJ 5856.*

Opposite top: One of the lesser parts of the Great Western system was the loop from West Ealing and Hanwell on the main line, to the High Wycombe line at Greenford. There were three intermediate stations; this is South Greenford Halt on 9 March 1968, looking north towards Greenford. The term 'Halt' was deleted from the name a year later, in 1969. This is a typical Great Western structure for an unstaffed stopping place, with a pagoda style waiting room. It was opened on 20 September 1926. Entrance to the station platform for passengers would have been from the far end. The platform ramp for railway staff is decidedly minimal and looks likely to be slippery in wet weather. There are however four lighting columns for electric lamps. The station is built somewhat precariously (as it later turned out) on an embankment. In much more recent times this gave way, taking part of the platform with it and leaving only that on the other side of the line. For a time, passengers from here to the stations of Castle Bar Park, Drayton Green, West Ealing and Ealing Broadway had to start by travelling in the opposite direction to Greenford, stay on the train, and return. Or they could walk to Castle Bar Park. Services in those days between Ealing Broadway and Greenford Central Line (shown thus in the timetable entry) were up to three an hour in the peak, dropping to hourly for the rest of the day. There was no Sunday service. The end to end journey time was 13 minutes for the 3½ miles. Passenger usage at South Greenford in 2018/19 (entries plus exits) was a decidedly modest 28,000. *Ref. AAJ 6035.*

This page bottom: The construction of the Central line extension to West Ruislip, opened to Greenford in 1947, also resulted in the Great Western local services along the main line to High Wycombe and the stations served becoming superfluous. However, the branch from Ealing Broadway still had to be accommodated. The new island platform at Greenford station for the Underground thus incorporated a central bay at the London end for these trains. Latterly the shuttle service provided was (and is) provided by a diesel unit. On 5 September 1959, one such train is seen approaching that platform, which has a four car capacity. The line rises from a junction with the then existing line, as the route was still needed for other traffic. As can be seen, the Central line tracks rise to cross the lower level route. Signalling on the Great Western lines was by lower quadrant semaphores, notably for exit from the Greenford platform, but also on the left of this picture for what was then the main line from Paddington to Birmingham Snow Hill and indeed to Birkenhead Woodside (closed 1967). The Underground signalling was by colour lights. *Ref. AAJ 4208.*

Top: The main line look of the British Railways part of Greenford can be seen in this view of 19 March 1955. This shows one of the two Great Western Streamlined Parcels Cars, No. W34W, on the down main line heading towards High Wycombe. It is in British Railways overall dark red livery, as used on parcels vehicles generally. The railcar design dated from 1932 and a total of 38 were built over the succeeding decade. These were to a number of designs for passenger services, for a variety of tasks. They were also sourced from various manufacturers. Nearly all were double ended enabling them to work as single units, but one pair were built single ended, meaning that they were worked back to back and incorporated buffet facilities. The other vehicle built as a Parcels car was W17W. The idea behind this was that too many parcels on ordinary services resulted in an unacceptable increase in station stop times, and dedicated parcels cars was an effective way of tackling the problem. In 1955, the 33 surviving cars were allocated as follows: Bristol 5, Gloucester 1, Landore 1, Leamington 1, Newport 2, Oxford 4, Reading 4, Southall 5, Stourbridge 3, Weymouth 1, Worcester 6. The last was withdrawn in 1962. The remains

of the British Railways Greenford station are just visible. It saw only occasional use after 1949 when the Central line (in the background at a higher level) was fully open, and was closed altogether in 1963. *Ref. AAJ 1827.*

Bottom: The West London line and its extension had a mixed history in terms of local services and intermediate stations. For most of the post-war years, there was but one stopping place, Kensington Olympia. The only regular service ran twice in each direction in both the morning and evening peaks, Mondays to Fridays, from Clapham Junction. This was for Post Office Savings Bank workers. It was sometimes advertised as available to the public, sometimes not. There was also the ubiquitous District line Underground service. This usually ran as a shuttle to and from High Street, Kensington, mainly for the benefit of visitors to the Olympia exhibition centre. Other stations on the line had been closed, including Chelsea & Fulham, a street view of which is seen here on Saturday 21 April 1956. Remarkably, closure had taken place in Autumn 1940 due to enemy action, but it was still in presentable condition. The station opened in 1865 and in the background may be seen Battersea Power Station, the terminus of the coming Northern line extension. In the station forecourt is a remarkable collection of cars. It is notable that there is no sign of white lines to indicate parking bays, so this seems likely to have been a special occasion of some nature. The station was close to the Chelsea Football Club ground at Stamford Bridge. *Ref. AAJ 2322.*

National Rail, Southern

One of the many examples of 4-SUB units is seen here arriving from Chessington South into Platform 2 at Waterloo in the early afternoon of 28 June 1969. By their positioning, the waiting passengers are clearly expecting a four car formation, and they have lined themselves up with the similar four car train on Platform 3. They are also not standing too close to the buffer stops. This is the main line suburban side of Waterloo, i.e. not including the Windsor lines, trains for which leave from the high number platforms over the far side of the concourse. The 4-SUB term was an all-embracing category for what the Ian Allan ABCs managed to categorise into 24 different types plus a further seven sub-types. They were built from 1925 onwards, initially as three car units, later strengthened to four cars. But many of the vehicles were not new then, being converted variously from steam stock constructed by the Southern Railway constituent companies. The number of seats on what were nominally the same type of compartment stock unit varied enormously, from 340 to 468. Different vehicle lengths and hence the number of compartments accounted for some of this, but also the class of travel for which they were constructed. Those in the know could select the most commodious former First Class vehicles; their seat spacing gave them the nickname of the 'ballroom dancing' type. At the other end of the scale were those known as the 'interlocking knees' versions. This set is from one of the 10 post-war builds (or rebuilds). By the mid-1950s, there were 359 4-SUBs. Broadly similar vehicles built from 1951 onwards were termed 4-EPBs (or 2-EPBs). Most were to last until the arrival of sliding door stock; Waterloo services then received 43 Class 508 trains, the production versions of the experimental PEP trains, from 1979. These were later sent to Merseyrail, to be replaced by the Class 455 series of units from 1982. They were still in service in 2020. *Ref. AAJ 6283.*

Splendid mechanical informative devices of this nature used to be commonplace at major stations. There was a series of whirrs and clunks as the staff rotated the individual station names after the train concerned left, or a new departure was added. This was the main departure indicator at Waterloo, seen here after mid-day on Saturday 28 June 1969. It covers departures, separately, for Suburban Services, Portsmouth & Isle of Wight, Aldershot & Alton, Winchester, Southampton, Bournemouth & Weymouth, plus Andover, Salisbury & West of England. Another indicator on the far side of the concourse was used for Windsor line services. Traditionally, Waterloo had four key types of special traffic: those attending the races at Ascot, Epsom, Esher (Sandown Park) and Kempton Park, Army and Navy personnel to Aldershot, Andover, Salisbury, Portsmouth and Plymouth, special ocean liner trains to Southampton and the holidaymakers. Large contingents of commuters were a later addition. Such mechanical devices were impressive, but were not without problems. Thus we see the 13:47 to Bournemouth appears to call at Brockenhurst, Lymington, New Milton and so on. But for those who know, Lymington is on a dead end branch. Cue to read the stern notice at the top of the display: 'Passengers should enquire at the platform barrier if and where a change is necessary.' What if the same train appears in more than one section? Thus under Aldershot & Alton, the rear portion of the 13:43 from Platform 4 calls at Surbiton, Woking, stations to Alton and stations then to Itchen Abbas, from which it might be expected to continue to Winchester. But under the Winchester etc group there is another 13:43, apparently first stop Winchester, then Southampton, Brockenhurst, and stations to Bournemouth. This too is billed as leaving from Platform 4. They can't both be completely right! Similarly, there is a 13:23 to Portsmouth and a 13:53 to Alton. A separate sign at the bottom reads 'This train calls at Wimbledon'. But which one, or is it both? Queuing instructions at the top are on a separate display. These differentiated between those with reserved seats, and the chancers – the unreserved. *Ref. AAJ 6282.*

The camera catches the old main line booking office at Waterloo on its last day of operation on 5 December 1970. A separate office dealt with tickets for local travel. Ticket issuing can be a complicated business. Particularly with local services, many passengers will know precisely what they want and put the exact money down on the counter as they ask. Others will be much less sure, with long distance in particular. 'When is my train?' 'Which platform?' 'Do I have to change trains?' 'Is there a buffet car?' Worst of all, 'I didn't think it would be as much as that, I'll have to write you a cheque', fumble, fumble … then, eventually, 'Can I use your pen?' In those days, cash was king, credit cards were in their infancy, while ticket machines for other than the most basic journeys were non-existent. The willingness to stand in long queues to buy tickets is also probably rather less than it was but, on the other hand, penalty fares discourage people from just trying their luck with the ticket barriers. And if you don't have enough time to buy a ticket, whose fault is that? The London Regional Passengers' Committee have produced guidelines on how long it was reasonable to expect people to wait in a queue. Today, pre-purchase of tickets is more common, as is storing them on mobile devices. Various rail companies have their own cards. Ticket machines are far more versatile in what they can offer, though the less frequent traveller is easily baffled. 'How do I decide which route I want if it gives me a choice?' 'How do I get the machine to give me a Railcard discount?' 'Can I use an Oystercard?' The human presence can still be very important.
Ref. AAJ 6658.

It is 12:20 at Waterloo on summer Saturday 31 August 1968. The holiday crowds are out in force, well encumbered with suitcases. They are not milling aimlessly around, but congregating under one of the displayed letters above their heads telling them where to wait. The blackboard display for Queue A, nearest the camera, says that it is for those without reservations travelling to Guildford, Havant, Portsmouth & Southsea and Portsmouth Harbour for the Isle of Wight. A partially visible painted white line indicates where people were supposed to wait. Holiday traffic was then an important feature of this part of the railway on summer Saturdays, given the propensity of the seaside landladies to take only Saturday to Saturday bookings. Coastal destinations were the most popular, probably in Hampshire, Dorset or the Isle of Wight, but also perhaps Devon. The branch to Swanage was still there, though it was to close in 1972, but that to Lyme Regis had already gone in 1965 and that to Seaton in 1966. Further west, services to Ilfracombe were to cease in 1970 whilst those to Bude, 1966, and Padstow, 1967, were already no more. Summer Saturday traffic was not an unalloyed blessing; in 1963 Dr Beeching claimed that throughout the country 6,000 coaches kept for seasonal traffic at the high peak were used on average on only 14 occasions a year. The annual cost of providing them was £3.4 million, against which the revenue was £0.5 million. Much of the Waterloo summer traffic was provided by trains which had year-round use, but a substantial number did not. *Ref. AAJ 6128.*

Top: In this view, looking towards Waterloo, the train on which the photographer is travelling is approaching from Reading, and will couple up to the waiting train originating from Guildford, in Platform 1. Ascot is the junction for the two lines, that to Aldershot and Guildford diverges to the right of the picture taken on 27 August 1966. Over the years different views have been taken on whether to provide through services from both routes by joining and splitting trains, or whether to make some through passengers change. Ascot is the station for the famous racecourse, which accounts for the extensive facilities seen here, though these were subsequently reduced to three platforms only. With slam doors, passengers could join and alight from trains on both sides, as here using Platforms 1 and 2. This could make interchange much easier for the passenger, but such facilities are no longer available with sliding door stock. The platforms here are connected by subway, rather than a bridge. There is a fine array of semaphore signals, with a Southern 'Odeon' style box to the right and a traditional box just visible at the other end of the station. *Ref. AAJ 5800.*

Bottom: Bracknell New Town in Berkshire was so designated in 1949; previously it has been described as a village-cum-small town. It has long had a station on the London & South Western Railway, opened on 9 July 1856, with the electrification through here to Reading completed in 1939. This is a view towards London Waterloo, taken on 27 August 1966. Bracknell then had a typical wayside station look about it, with two side platforms, a signal box (with the semaphores pulled off in both directions), an end loading dock on the left, plus a goods yard mostly out of sight. The end of one of two sidings can be seen on the right; these were for holding goods trains awaiting access to Reading. In the foreground there is a sleeper crossing for staff use; the passenger footbridge is at the far end of the platforms. Bracknell New Town had a planned population of 25,000, upped to 60,000 in the late 1960s. It is now around 84,000. The traditional station seen here was swept away in 1975 and the up side buildings were replaced by a modern office block on the up platform, with station facilities at platform level. The goods yard had already closed, in 1969. *Ref. AAJ 5799.*

Above: A curious oddment of railway operation remains on the Surrey/ Hampshire border, centred on Aldershot, seen here on 3 July 1971. A 4-COR unit No. 3140 is in the course of reversing with a Guildford-Aldershot-Ascot train. These trains were intended for the Portsmouth main line electrification of 1937 and a total of 58 units with 30 First and 196 Second class seats were built. Later demoted to more menial tasks, these local trains served Guildford, Wanborough, Ash, Aldershot, Ash Vale, Frimley, Camberley, Bagshot and Ascot. The end-to-end distance is 20¼ miles, with the total time taken an unexciting 60 minutes. Besides the wish to make whatever connections were reasonably possible at Guildford, Aldershot and Ascot, the usual junction conflicts have to be contended with in the timetabling, plus a single track section for a couple of miles between Ash Vale and Frimley. Besides that, the route via Aldershot adds about four miles to the direct distance between Ash Vale and Ash (not available by rail). Should perhaps these trains run via Farnham as well as Aldershot? Perhaps, but this is another 11 miles return added to the journey, which translates into 10 or so minutes of extra running time. Or break the service at Aldershot so that it becomes two separate services? *Ref. AAJ 6732.*

Opposite top: Vauxhall station is 1 mile 29 chains from London Waterloo, and an often used spot from which to view passing trains. This is 8 July 1967 and sees an unidentified Class 73 electro-diesel locomotive approaching on the down fast line with a train formed of a 4-TC unit. These were conversions of existing MkI coaching stock and were built so that the Bournemouth electrification could take place on the cheap. Unpowered themselves, the TC units were equipped with driving cabs at each end. The normal means of operation was for one (or more usually two) of them to be propelled from Waterloo to Bournemouth by a high powered 4-REP straight electric unit. These too were mostly conversions. At Bournemouth, a Class 33 diesel would come on to the front end and it would then take either one or both TC units on to Poole and Weymouth.These would then be propelled back to Bournemouth and an eight or 12 car train reassembled, to return to Waterloo. In that way, the cost of another 60 miles of electrification was avoided - until the REP+TC+TC combinations wore out. Meanwhile the Class 73s proved themselves as versatile locomotives, particularly for freight. As seen here, this train will be electrically powered, but it could also continue on to non-electrified lines, from Worting Junction (Basingstoke) to Salisbury, for instance. No headcode was being displayed. *Ref. AAJ 5980.*

Bottom: There are four platforms at Wimbledon set aside for District line services; this is the ticket barrier for Platforms 1 and 2 on 15 January 1966. The R stock train on the right has evidently just arrived. This picture illustrates how much a manned ticket barrier limits the speed of a crowd, especially if there are those trying to join a train as well. Is it better to have barriers for the whole station together, or separately for Underground and British Railways, or even more separately for each pair of platforms? How many railway passengers alight here for interchange only, rather than leaving the station? Revenue protection is certainly one goal, but so too are keeping staffing costs under control and keeping people moving. Note too the rather crude system of indicating the waiting time for the next train, and also the indicator as to whether the train is for Edgware Road (Platform 1), or Mansion House (Platform 2). Mansion House is no longer possible as a terminating point, as the facilities have been removed, as indeed have those at Whitechapel. Note too the timetable display on the left. In Platform 1 can be seen a CO/CP stock train, shorter than the R stock, and so suitable for the shorter platforms found on the Edgware Road route. Ref. *AAJ 5629.*

57

Left: The ticket hall at Wimbledon was photographed on 16 July 1966. There are two windows for 'Southern' and two for 'Underground' (one of which is hidden). The portable poster stand tells passengers that on Mondays 0730-0915 Weekly tickets will be issued only at the enquiry office (on the right of the picture) to ease queues at the Southern windows. In those days, weekly season tickets were only valid for the set week, Monday to Sunday, and Monday mornings could be very busy indeed for the ticket office staff. Such tickets took a good bit longer to issue than 'ordinaries', as they also had to be stamped with the expiry date and the week number, plus a 'W' stamp if issued to a female. Those in the know who had tickets for the previous week could renew them from the previous Friday evening, which was much easier for all concerned. Nowadays, such tickets can be for any seven consecutive days. But for those who could afford it, a monthly or longer period ticket worked out a good deal cheaper. A passenger operated ticket machine, to the left, offered a single fare to Waterloo, 7¼ miles, for 2s 3d (11p) The seat in the middle of the ticket hall seemed to be well used; in those days the space was not needed for banks of self-service ticket machines. Wimbledon station was owned and operated by the Southern Region of British Rail; the District line of the Underground was a secondary user. Then, as now, the station platforms did not carry Underground roundels. *Ref. AAJ 5682.*

Opposite bottom: 4-SUB No. 4753 is seen on an up local service to London Waterloo as it calls at Raynes Park's Platform 2 on 19 September 1970. The island platforms here are highly staggered. This is to allow for the up trains from Epsom (and Chessington), which have passed under the main lines to call at Platform 1 on the other side of the far island, while down trains use Platform 3 as shown here for the main line, or branch to Platform 4 (out of picture, right) for Epsom. As General Manager of the Southern Railway, and the London & South Western Railway before that, (Sir) Herbert Walker was very alive to the benefits that grade separated junctions could bring. In the whole of the South Western main line suburban area, the only notable omission was where the Portsmouth line diverges from the main line immediately to the west of Woking station. The track layout of up slow, up fast, down fast, down slow is beneficial in that trains going in the same direction can be switched from one track to the other relatively easily, but it is less helpful at terminals. The flyover east of Wimbledon changes this to up fast, down fast, up slow, down slow. Thus in the run up to Waterloo the fast trains are kept together and so are the slow trains. This much benefits their positioning for the return journey. *Ref. AAJ 6612.*

Above: 4-CIG (Class 421/2) No. 7337 takes the down fast line through Surbiton on 19 September 1970 with a semi-fast train from Waterloo to Portsmouth Harbour. Note the Jackson bag in the foreground! Surbiton station was moved from a site further east to the present site in 1845. It had various names, settling on Surbiton in 1867. The name changes reflect its origins. The London & South Western Railway line was originally to be routed via Kingston, but the town objected so a more southerly route was taken. As a result, Kingston only got a branch railway, and then not until 1863. Surbiton station was comprehensively rebuilt by the Southern Railway in 1937. It was designed by the company's Chief Architect James Robb Scott. The style is Art Deco and it was given Grade II listed status in 1983. It is considered generally to be one of the best (if not the best) of its type and very little has since changed. Ground to overbridge lifts, provided originally for parcels traffic, are now available for passenger use. There are two, long, island platforms. Entry can be effected from both the up side (main entrance) or the down side. The down side used to feature a small goods yard, but this was closed in 1971. Its site is now occupied by the station car park and some residential flats. Scott originally designed the station to have a bold 'Southern Railway' name above the main entrance, but this was removed (or gradually removed itself) during the 1980s. On refurbishment c1990, the British Rail architect involved wanted to restore the heading, but 'Southern Railway' was no longer correct or appropriate. He therefore devised a new inscription of 'Surbiton Station' in the same size and style as the original. This, he calculated, used the same number of letters and should therefore look right. Few would disagree with his conclusion. *Ref. AAJ 6613.*

Above: From their introduction in 1964, the 90mph 4-VEP units (Vestibuled Electro Pneumatic brake) and later Class 423 were the mainstay of outer-suburban Southern Region routes. In total, 194 units were built. Their final withdrawal in 2005 was prompted by the increasing concern over the safety of external slam doors. Here, unit No. 7782 is approaching Surbiton on the up slow line with a stopping service from Portsmouth & Southsea to London Waterloo on 19 September 1970. The all blue livery, it may be said, did not suit them, and the later change to blue and grey was a considerable improvement. Seating for Second Class passengers was in the open saloons in the tightly spaced and hard seated 3+2 variety, but First Class passengers were treated to compartments, each seating six. There were four such compartments in each of the driving end vehicles. Later in their career, it was decided that some of these compartments would be downgraded to Second Class, and it became an unseemly scramble to find out which these might be and make a spirited run for them. A variation was the conversion of 12 trains of VEP stock, for the Rapid City Link service for Gatwick Airport. In each set, 24 seats were hauled out and replaced by luggage racks. Perhaps inevitably, these became 4-VEG units. They were replaced by Class 73 hauled Gatwick Express air-conditioned sets in 1984. *Ref. AAJ 6614.*

Opposite top: The expansion of the London suburbs in the inter-war period must have seemed that it would go on for ever. In many ways, this is indeed what happened, until the advent of war in 1939 put an end to house building for the time being. It was in such circumstances that the Southern Railway decided to build a new route between Motspur Park and Leatherhead. This would serve the new housing, but also relieve the existing route to Wimbledon and Waterloo via Epsom, the trains on which were increasingly becoming overcrowded. Thus this new line was to be built as a diversionary through route, which would also generate its own traffic. Motspur Park station was opened on 20 September 1925 (or thereabouts, sources vary) and remained unaltered when the Chessington branch was built. Unusually, the only public access was by the footbridge shown; there was, and is, no step free route. At the bottom of the central steps, facing away from the camera, was the ticket office. There is only the central island platform, with neither bays nor side platforms; the Chessington branch was always to be served by a through service from London Waterloo. In this picture, 4-EPB unit No. 5125 is arriving on 16 June 1973 with a headcode 18 train, meaning its destination is Chessington South. *Ref. AAJ 7122.*

The Chessington line left that to Epsom 34 chains south of Motspur Park station, at Motspur Park Junction. This curved away to the south west and is just about visible in this view of 16 June 1973. But first there was a level crossing with traditional swing gates, and the controlling signal box of London & South Western Railway design. Level crossings are a curse of railway operation, and road users are not fond of them either. At this crossing, using 2020 service levels, the off-peak service consisted of two trains per hour to Chessington and four to Epsom (straight ahead) or beyond. So taking account of journeys in the reverse direction, that amounts to 12 crossing closures for perhaps several minutes per hour, and more in the peak. Sometimes up and down trains will cross each other here, and each time that happens it makes for one fewer closure. However, closures with two trains involved are also likely to last longer. To complicate matters further, there is another level crossing half a mile nearer London (behind the camera), where similar considerations apply. There are no level crossings on the Chessington branch itself. *Ref. AAJ 7121.*

Opposite top: All four branch stations have similar architecture, but while the first two to be opened (Malden Manor and Tolworth, 29 May 1938) have main buildings of concrete, the latter two (Chessington North and Chessington South, 28 May 1939) were of brick. Chessington North is seen from street level in this photograph of 16 June 1973, in full British Rail regalia, but long before the creation of Network SouthEast. All the stations feature side platforms on a double track formation and the rounded and stylish Art Deco design was created for the Southern Railway by their architect, James Robb Scott. There was a ticket office in the spacious entrance hall and the position of the staircase for (in this case) down trains from Waterloo to Chessington South is clearly visible. There was also a lift tower at each station to be used in connection with parcels traffic to be conveyed by train, but no lifts were installed before World War II and in the event all remain unused. All branch stations also have nearby bus stops for onward travel. *Ref. AAJ 7127.*

Opposite bottom: This is Chessington South on 3 March 1962 and all is not well. There are two platforms, but there is no access to the nearer one for passengers. A bricked up opening in the main building shows where the connecting bridge was to have been built. The up platform, as such it would have been, has never had a bridge to connect it, and has remained unused. The problem after World War II was not only lack of finance and resources, but the new Green Belt legislation. This effectively prohibited the development of much land around the large cities, and that between Chessington and Leatherhead came into this category. In this way, the hopes of the Southern Railway and their British Railways successors were thwarted. No housing meant no potential passenger traffic, therefore no railway was required. Development south of this station is negligible. Construction work had thus ceased for good and the situation today is unchanged. Thoughts in the 1990s that the line might be extended to the development site formerly occupied by the Epsom mental hospitals came to nothing, and the originally intended route to Leatherhead has been obstructed by the construction of the M25 Motorway. *Ref. AAJ 4532.*

Above: Other branch stations are above ground level, but Chessington South station is in a cutting. 4-EPB unit (Class 415/1) No. 5118 is seen here from the road bridge south of the station on 16 June 1973; the red blind on what is now the rear of the train takes the place of a tail light to confirm that the train is complete. The line continued for a short distance beyond, but only to give access to sidings. Latterly these formed a Coal Concentration Depot for the economical distribution of domestic coal over a wider area, but this traffic evaporated in the 1980s. The track on the left, which would have formed the up line was electrified, but its use was to stable a spare train should that be needed. The extra track can also be used for a run-round for locomotives with engineering trains. The whole of the half hourly passenger service can be run to and from the only operational platform on the right. Of note are the Chisarc platform canopies to be found at all branch stations. This cantilevered, reinforced concrete roofing has small circular glass lenses let into it, to give lighting by day. The same feature was used over the stairways. However, its value was negated by Railtrack who, around the turn of the century, painted over the glass as well as the concrete. For night use, fluorescent lighting was fitted, quite an advance in the late 1930s. *Ref. AAJ 7128.*

Opposite: This picture of 16 September 1967 shows, in the distance and at a higher level, Morden South station, with the usual platform canopy and waiting area of the Wimbledon & Sutton stations. It was opened on 5 January 1930. In the foreground is the covered shed of the Sutton Express Dairy plant, which undertook the bottling, testing and distribution of milk and milk products to 125 depots around London. The milk arrived, partly by road but also by rail in 3,000 gallon capacity milk tanks. The milk was sourced from the West Country and was tripped from Acton, with access to the private sidings from the Sutton direction. These had a 14 wagon capacity. They also had to cope with 16ton mineral wagons, as seen here, as the plant, opened in 1954, was coal fired until 1972. Subsequent oil supplies came in by road. Shunting was in the hands of a Ruston & Hornsby four-wheeled diesel mechanical unit, replaced by Hunslet Yardmaster *David* in 1972. Further details of the plant can be found on line in a promotional Express Dairy 1950s film *The Daily Round in the Story of Milk Production and Distribution*, in which it was claimed that this was the fastest dairy service in the world. Rail usage ceased in 1978 and the plant itself closed in 1992. The site is now occupied by a very large mosque. The site was between the end of the sidings at Morden Northern line depot and the Wimbledon & Sutton line. Was the building of a station here a good move for the Southern Railway? Recent figures show the annual number of passenger entries and exits combined at the nearby Morden Underground, opened 13 September 1926, as being in excess of 10 million. By contrast, according to the Office of Rail & Road, Morden South managed a mere 68,000 in 2018/19. *Ref. AAJ 6003.*

Above: The Southern Railway and their predecessors were always keen to defend their territory from other companies which might wish to encroach onto it. Thus the District Railway certainly had ambitions in terms of an extension of its Wimbledon branch to Sutton, though how this might cross the South Western main line was a major physical hurdle. A flat junction was out of the question, which left either a viaduct or tunnelling. Meanwhile, the Underground's Northern line had reached Clapham Common in 1900, and further extension was clearly on the cards. In the end, Morden was to be the permanent end for the Underground, the District stayed at Wimbledon, and the Southern constructed the Wimbledon & Sutton line. It was opened in two phases, from Wimbledon as far as South Merton on 7 July 1929 and thence to Sutton on 5 January 1930. This view taken on 6 August 1963 shows the front of Wimbledon Chase station from the road. The architecture has distinct similarities to the (considerably later) stations on the Chessington branch, even to the extent of the tower for a never installed parcels lift. *Ref. AAJ 4920.*

Top: Sutton Common station entrance, seen here on 6 August 1963, was never more than a minimalist station. Opened 5 January 1930, as with others on this two track branch, it was built with 520ft platforms, sufficient for eight car trains. It is unstaffed, there are ticket machine and telephones, loudspeaker announcements, and arrival and departure screens. There are steps to the island platform, which has passenger shelters. Has the line been a successful venture? First, it appears to have been built down to a price, not up to a standard. But the real problem is perhaps that journeys to and from central London are decidedly slow. Journey times between City Thameslink and a mid-point on the Wimbledon & Sutton are 45-50 minutes, depending on whether you travel via Wimbledon or via Sutton. From Waterloo to Wimbledon itself, by comparison, takes 16 minutes, including three intermediate stops, and trains are frequent. As a result, usage is relatively light. Service frequency, at half hourly, is about as low as it can be for a true electric suburban service. Transport for London have plans for a vaguely parallel link by London Tramlink, the progress of which will be watched with interest. *Ref. AAJ 4927.*

Opposite bottom: West Sutton station was opened on 5 January 1930 and this view shows that which greeted the would be passenger. Alan Jackson himself referred to it as a blockhouse. This is a term of military origin, referring to a small fortification. Functional it may have been, attractive to modern eyes it is not. In this picture of 6 August 1963, the remains of previous inscriptions on the concrete may be seen, though the main interest is perhaps the Southern sign, displayed on a British Railways double sausage creation above the entrance. Like other intermediate stations on the Wimbledon & Sutton, facilities have been reduced over the years, and all now have the status of unstaffed halts. There

is stepped access from street to the island platform, which has passenger shelters, and not much else. The line has been known unkindly by railway people as the 'Wall of Death'. This is no reference to its accident record, but to its physical features. Essentially, there is considerable curvature throughout, limiting maximum train speeds, and the land rises by about 150 feet in the journey from Wimbledon to Sutton. The *pièce de résistance* are the triple reverse curves over the mile from West Sutton to Sutton, with a gradient at a maximum of 1 in 44, through a cutting lined with concrete. The journey takes three minutes. Such are the problems of building a new surface railway through an area which has already been developed. *Ref. AAJ 4928.*

This page: London Victoria is among the top stations on National Rail for passenger volumes, as measured by the annual entries plus exits. In 2018/19, this accounted for 75 million people. This view is of the Brighton company's side of the concourse on 18 September 1970, more specifically Platforms 9 to 17 only. The departure indicator confines itself to the Brighton line's trains. Those looking for trains to Kent and in those days boat trains for sailings to France, have to walk to the Chatham side of the station, Platforms 1 to 8, and the indicator there. In this picture, the sign for Gentlemen refers also to the Showers & Hairdressing Saloon adjacent to Platform 2. This was perhaps a sought after facility for those arriving with bleary eyes off the then still extant Night Ferry service from Paris. Inner suburban trains used mostly Platforms 9 to 12 and the ornate entrance to Platform 12 may be seen. Cunningly hidden away around the corner, those wanting longer distance trains starting from Platforms 16 and 17 will still have quite a walk. Of long gone attractions, the Cartoon Cinema, directions as indicated, would at any rate amuse the children for an hour or so. *Ref. AAJ 6605.*

Top: On 15 September 1963 a special train left Victoria. headed by the unique Caledonian Railway 4-2-2 No. 123, complete with whitewashed coal, and London & South Western Railway T9 class 4-4-0 No. 120. With the Blue Belle headboard, the locomotives took the train to Haywards Heath, where they were detached. They then ran light engine to Brighton. This enabled them to be turned on the still extant turntable in the former Motive Power Depot. Meanwhile the train itself was taken to Horsted Keynes and then Sheffield Park on the Bluebell Railway, using that railway's class 0415 Adams 4-4-2T and E4 class 0-6-2T Brighton locomotive No. 473 *Birch Grove*. Nos. 123 and 120 followed as light engines, and took the train on its return journey to Victoria. Here, they are seen passing Clapham Junction on the outward journey; the photographer was indeed fortunate that the 4-EPB suburban set No. 5050 was almost clear of the special's engines when they passed. It is interesting to record that in those days British Railways felt able to restore both locomotives to full operational condition at their own expense. Today, No. 123 is in the Glasgow Museum of Transport, while No. 120 may be found on the Swanage Railway. *Ref. AAJ 5000.*

Opposite bottom: The Southern Railway pioneered main line electrification in Britain, starting in 1933 with their line to Brighton. This was extended before World War II to Eastbourne, Littlehampton, Bognor Regis and Portsmouth Harbour. The Brighton Belle was their flagship train, seen here with 5-BEL unit No. 3052 in the traditional umber and cream Pullman livery heading a 10-car formation on the up fast line through Clapham Junction's Platform 12 on 16 July 1966. Trains left Victoria at 11.0 am, 3.0 pm and 7.0 pm, returning from Brighton at 1.25 pm, 5.25 pm and 8.25 pm. On Sundays, there were two journeys in each direction. All trains ran non-stop for the 60 minute and 50½ mile journey. It will be seen that one train could comfortably cover the whole service. There were three 5-BEL units, each made up of a Motor Brake Second Pullman (48 seats), a Trailer Second Pullman (56 seats), a Trailer Kitchen First Pullman (20 seats), a Trailer Kitchen First Pullman (20 seats), and a Motor Brake Second Pullman (48 seats). The total seating capacity was thus 192, made up of 40 First Class and 152 Second Class, not very many for a five car trains. 'It is desirable that 1st and 2nd class seats in the Pullman Cars … be reserved in advance by personal or postal application and payment of the supplementary fee.' In 1960 this was 3/- (15p) 1st class, or 2/- (10p) 2nd class. Meals and refreshments were served at every seat and were of course charged for extra, as was the fare for travel. The Brighton Belle, latterly in a grey and blue livery, survived until 1972. By then the vehicles were nearly 40 years old, albeit having been stored for the duration of World War II. *Ref. AAJ 5679.*

Below: Semaphore signals certainly add a touch of interest to the railway scene, even if wet as on 5 December 1965. This is the end of the down platform at Epsom, trains from which are given a choice of three routes from this rather splendid gantry. The signals allow trains to continue straight ahead to Leatherhead (the tallest of the three), left to the turnback siding which was also used for activities such as carriage cleaning, or right on to the up road. In both cases this was for terminating services, so that they could be reversed into one of the pair of up platforms for Waterloo or Victoria respectively. Semaphores may look attractive, but they do need a lot of maintenance. How visible are they under various lighting conditions? How are they lit at night? If the answer is oil the wicks need trimming and the oil replenished; if electric, where is the nearest supply of power? How are they controlled, mechanically or electrically? If mechanical, the signal box cannot be too far away, since the signaller will need brute strength in order to operate them. How are they interlocked with points and other signals, to ensure that contrary indications cannot be given? But the system is safe and backed up with many years of experience. It is however costly, particularly in staff time. *Ref. AAJ 5587.*

Above: Railway history has left some strange results. Thus the South Eastern Railway, whose route to Kent was via Redhill, also owned part of it. This was a serious frustration for the Brighton company in terms of track availability for their own services. The South Eastern also built a station on this line at Coulsdon South, which they opened on 1 October 1899. The Brighton had two answers, the principal one being to quadruple the railway but with the two additional tracks on a different alignment (the Quarry Line). Crucially, this would avoid Redhill and would be for their own exclusive use. This was opened on 5 November 1899, on the same date as their new station at Coulsdon North. This had two platforms on the Quarry line and two more as terminal platforms, with sidings beyond. There was yet another station serving the same area and owned by the South Eastern company. This was at Smitham on the Tattenham Corner branch, opened on 1 January 1904. Smitham was all but adjacent to Coulsdon North. The picture, taken on 3 October 1964, shows 4-SUB unit No. 4624 (Class 405) leaving the down Quarry line, passing Coulsdon North signal box, and entering one of the terminal platforms of Coulsdon North. The original line to Redhill is on the right. Such an arrangement was unlikely to last for ever, and Coulsdon North station was closed with the last train calling on Friday 30 September 1983. Smitham station was renamed Coulsdon Town on 22 May 2011. *Ref. AAJ 5378.*

Opposite top: Ashtead is the only station between Epsom and Leatherhead and is seen here on Sunday 8 March 1970. The job in hand is relaying the up track, and this scene is looking towards Leatherhead. The task here is unloading new ballast from a train of Grampus wagons, which were built in their thousands for use by the Civil Engineer's departments of British Railways. Designed to carry sleepers or ballast, these wagons had three sectioned drop down sides. This much enhanced the ability to load or unload them manually, as here. This is hard physical work, and it is of note that 25 or so men are visible. This excludes those carrying out related duties beyond the reach of the camera, not forgetting the locomotive crews and staff carrying out protection duties. There is also a fair amount of dust flying around the atmosphere. This is an electrified railway, and reinstatement of the track has to be accompanied by relaying the conductor rails, making good all electrical connections as necessary, and ensuring that the signalling system is in full working order. *Ref. AAJ 6454.*

Opposite bottom: This view of Ashtead station during relaying work on 8 March 1970 is taken from the footbridge, looking towards Epsom and London. At the end of the platform is a (fortunately) little used level crossing, though two young cyclists are wondering if and when they will be allowed to cross. It is under the control of the adjacent Ashtead signal box. The work being done is the movement of track panels in the traditional 60ft lengths. Over the years, this has been found to be a suitable size to both assemble and then store in depots, and then to move around by rail and install as necessary. Such panels are not by any stretch of the imagination lightweight, but handling them is well within the capabilities of the wagon mounted cranes seen in this picture. An essential part of such an operation is having some wagons available for their loading or unloading; both will be needed, as the old panels have to be removed before the new ones can be installed. That requires locomotive power; in this picture a Class 33 and an 08 are visible, while an unidentified locomotive will be in charge of the wagons on which the panels are stored. This is a Sunday, and everything will need to be back to normal by early Monday morning. *Ref. AAJ 6455.*

This page top: The Tooting, Merton and Wimbledon line opened on 1 October 1868, dividing at Tooting Junction. Trains on the northern part called at Haydons Road before continuing to Wimbledon, where they faced south west. This line was electrified in 1929 and is still in use today as part of Thameslink. The other route ran further south via Merton Abbey station, seen here on 19 August 1957 and not looking as if it had been closed for years. The line continued to Merton Park, where it joined the Wimbledon to West Croydon line. This section ended up at Wimbledon facing north east, in the same platforms. All was double track.The line was a joint enterprise between the Brighton and South Western companies, which gained access to Wimbledon and the City of London respectively. But why did they need two routes? This stemmed from the opportunities for profitable goods traffic, particularly from industries around Merton Abbey. However, the modest passenger service on the more southerly route was to be completely overshadowed by the opening in 1926 of Colliers Wood station on the Underground's Northern line. The last regular passenger services ran on 2 March 1929, never to return. The route was severed at the Tooting end in 1934, with freight access then being from Merton Park only. Goods traffic to serve private sidings continued, but the last train ran on 1 May 1975. Following this, the track was lifted. Today, the Wimbledon-Merton Park section is part of London Tramlink. *Ref. AAJ 3147.*

Opposite bottom: The Wimbledon to West Croydon (WimWon) line was never one of the star performers for the Southern Region; not the least of its problems was the end to end journey time of 19 minutes for the 6¼ miles with six intermediate stops. One train could not make two return journeys in the hour, while two trains might provide a half hourly service, but would spend a lot of the time doing nothing. An uneasy compromise of a train every 45 minutes evolved. This view of the line on 21 March 1964 shows the section of single track looking north west towards Mitcham Junction, with that station in the distance. The Wimbledon – West Croydon service had to use the same two platforms here as trains for Sutton via Hackbridge, so some conflict in timings and junction use was inevitable. The opportunity arose for the Wimbledon to West Croydon line to become part of a new light rail system. Two new platforms, to include a passing loop, would be built at Mitcham Junction to the left of the existing. A new flyover rising from the near end of the station platforms, crossing over trains on the line via Hackbridge, and descending again in the foreground, would keep the trams completely separate. The British Rail line closed on 1 June 1997, to be reopened as what was initially called Croydon Tramlink as part of the Wimbledon to New Addington Tramlink service on 10 May 2000. It was followed by those from Wimbledon to Elmers End on 29 May. Passenger journeys on London Tramlink as a whole reached a high of 30.4 million in 2014/15. *Ref. AAJ 5121.*

This page: Services in the Oxted area are rather fewer than they used to be. The date is 4 April 1959 and is seen from the signal box at the south end of the down platform. Fairburn Class 4 2-6-4 tank No. 42103 dating from 1945 is at the head of a Victoria to Tunbridge Wells West train. A water supply is available for locomotives that need it. This train will travel over the present line towards East Grinstead, but then via the now closed High Level station and route to Groombridge (and over what is now the preserve of the Spa Valley Railway) to its destination. On the right is a smartly turned out tank locomotive, a South Eastern & Chatham Class H 0-4-4T, with a two coach train of venerable stock. This will leave five minutes later, but take the route via Edenbridge Town to Ashurst, then to Groombridge and also terminate at Tunbridge Wells West. The more direct route taken by the tank locomotive was about 20 minutes faster to Groombridge and beyond. It may be noted that Tunbridge Wells West was the Brighton company's station and laid out on the grand scale complete with locomotive depot. The route thence to the constricted Tunbridge Wells Central, a South Eastern station and lacking much in the way of terminating facilities, was via a single track, part of which was in tunnel to Grove Junction and then over South Eastern metals. *Ref. AAJ 3847.*

Above: The 4¾ mile and double track branch from Haywards Heath to Horsted Keynes, with one intermediate station at Ardingly, was opened on 3 September 1883. Here, 2-BIL set No. 2117 is seen arriving on 10 July 1963. These units consisted of a Second Class Driving Motor Coach and a Composite Driving Trailer, with a lavatory in each vehicle. The line was electrified on 7 July 1935 as part of the Brighton main line scheme. Sadly, it did not prosper. Horsted Keynes station was over a mile from its village namesake, but the station did offer interchange with the East Grinstead and Lewes Railway, opened the previous year. For some inscrutable reason, the station was blessed with five platforms linked by subway. In later days the electric service used only Platform 2. This has had the result that Horsted Keynes station, now part of the Bluebell, is the largest on any British preserved railway. Electric services usually ran from Horsted Keynes to and from Seaford via Lewes, taking a little over an hour. Until the closure of the direct steam service via Sheffield Park, there were through trains to Lewes by two completely different routes. The main line branch service was withdrawn on 28 October 1963. The first mile of the branch from Haywards Heath is still used by Hanson Aggregates; the rest has been lifted. A long term goal of the Bluebell Railway is to restore services at least as far as Ardingly. In this photograph, the track looking south towards Lewes is still overgrown. The Bluebell Railway's first train ran on 7 August 1960, but only to Bluebell Halt, a makeshift stopping place south of Horsted Keynes. British Railways allowed their trains to use the east side of the station in 1961. *Ref. AAJ 4902.*

Opposite: British Railways originally closed the Horsted Keynes to East Grinstead line with effect from 15 June 1955, though the last trains ran on 29 May due to strike action. But they reckoned without the intervention of Margery Bessemer, a resident of Chailey. This lady consulted the line's authorising Acts of 1887 and 1888 and discovered that they were obliged the railway to run four passenger trains from end to end, each way, daily, with stops at Horsted Keynes, West Hoathly, Sheffield Park and Newick & Chailey. This section of the legislation had not been annulled. So it was with bad grace that British Railways restored the service, with effect from 7 August 1956. What became known as the 'sulky service' was indeed just that. It consisted of the specified four train service, all running in the middle day period, but not calling at the other stations of Kingscote or Barcombe, as the Act did not mention them. Such a service was of little use to any would be users. British Railways did get their way in the end, although this involved Parliament repealing the legislation concerned. This view was taken from the 12:28 train from East Grinstead to Lewes as it approached West Hoathly station on Saturday 15 March 1958, the last day of operation before its second, formal closure on Monday 17 March 1958. Beyond the locomotive can be seen the 780 yard Sharpthorne Tunnel. There was however a spin off. The whole event gained sufficient publicity to galvanise the preservation movement to form what would eventually become the Bluebell Railway. This was the first standard gauge railway of its kind and is now operational over 11 miles of route between East Grinstead and Sheffield Park. West Hoathly station has not been reopened. *Ref. AAJ 3264.*

This page top: The first train of pre-1938 Underground stock destined for the Isle of Wight route from Ryde Pier Head to Shanklin is being prepared for external painting in Rail Blue at Stewarts Lane on 4 June 1966. A mixed bag of London Underground stock of varying vintages but all at least 30 years old had been selected for island service. At its peak in 1900, the Isle of Wight's railway network consisted of 55½ route miles, quite an achievement for an island of only 150 square miles and a population then of around 80,000. But it did not last, and by 1964 that network was down to 24¾ route miles, from Ryde to Shanklin and Ventnor, and Ryde to Newport and Cowes. Would the Minister of Transport agree to total closure? Eventually, the decision came that the 8½ miles of route between Ryde Pier Head and Shanklin must stay, but the rest could go. British Rail decided that electrification was the best

available option, with the use of former Underground stock the least costly. This also overcame the dimensional limitations posed by Ryde Esplanade tunnel, all 391 yards of it. The tunnel was prone to flooding and was to have its track bed raised. The steam services on the Cowes line ceased from 21 February 1966 and Shanklin to Ventnor from 18 April 1966. Electrification work began, and these services were inaugurated on 20 March 1967. They used a fleet of 43 cars of pre-1938 stock in formations of up to seven cars. The first UG stock sent to the Island was retired and replaced from 1989 by Underground 1938 stock. At about 80 years old, they in turn almost literally fell to pieces. They are to be superseded by a fleet of five two-car Class 230 trains of D stock, used formerly on the District line. In best island tradition, these too will be 40 years old by the time they arrive. *Ref. AAJ 5673 .*

Opposite bottom: This photograph shows the remains of the long defunct station of Ludgate Hill, closed on 2 March 1929, as it was on 12 July 1955. It was taken from the Blackfriars station platforms. The locomotive in the picture would appear to be a 4-4-0 of the D class or one of the derivative builds, which originated on the South Eastern & Chatham. The line represented the London,

Chatham & Dover Railway's attempt to gain a City, as well as a west end terminus (the Chatham side of Victoria). Their first temporary station was south of the River Thames at Blackfriars Bridge. The river was bridged in 1864 and Ludgate Hill station was established. This was the first permanent station, opened on 1 June 1865, on a route which would eventually meet the Metropolitan Railway's Widened Lines in the Farringdon area. Ludgate Hill station was rebuilt extensively in 1907, when two perilously narrow island platforms, only 17ft across, were replaced by one only, on the Snow Hill lines. That was 32ft across. It was very close to the present Blackfriars, opened on a new parallel alignment and with a second railway bridge (the present survivor) on 10 May 1886. According to the Railway Clearing House diagrams of 1903, the distance between the centre lines of the two stations was a mere eight chains, or 176 feet. During the 1920s, the local traffic ebbed away due to Underground and tram competition. Ludgate Hill station was closed in 1929, but remained as a derelict shell for many years. *Ref. AAJ 2002.*

Above: Opened as Snow Hill on 1 August 1874 but renamed Holborn Viaduct Low Level on 1 May 1912, this is what remained of this station when looking south on 10 September 1958. The withdrawal of local passenger services resulted in this station no longer being required and it was closed permanently on 1 June 1916. The tunnel itself remained busy with freight traffic until the 1960s, but this ceased altogether in 1962. The line then lay derelict until 1971, when the track was lifted. However unlikely it may have seemed at the time, this was not the end. The then Greater London Council had ambitions for the restoration of rail services and these came to fruition in 1988 with what might be termed Thameslink MkI. It saw the replacement of the Class 317 fleet of 25kV ac trains on the Bedford-St Pancras service with basically similar but dual voltage Class 319s and the introduction of services such as Bedford to Brighton. In the rush hours, the Moorgate services continued. That resulted in St Pancras station catering only for a modest offering of long distance services (Nottingham, Sheffield) and the overhead electrification there becoming surplus to requirements. The whole place began to look rather sad. Thirty years later, Thameslink has become a major player in cross-London movements with services to the Great Northern as well as the Midland lines, plus a variety of destinations south of London. Meanwhile, St Pancras main line station also deals with International trains and medium distance services to and from Kent. *Ref. AAJ 3675.*

Holborn Viaduct was the rather unprepossessing City terminal for the London, Chatham & Dover Railway. The company were authorised by Act of 1871 to build this short branch from their through City Line (so called) and it was opened on 2 March 1874. It is seen from the front of an incoming train on 16 July 1966. Of note are the varying lengths of the six platforms, later reduced to three. This was the result of a very confined site which had made an allowance for short trains only, the decline of parcels traffic of which there had been considerable volumes, and the desire to run longer trains where possible. The Southern Railway's progressive electrification schemes saw the need for steam traction at Holborn Viaduct eliminated in 1939. Out of sight to the left are the lines which dive below ground to meet at Farringdon with the Widened Lines. These would offer the Chatham company another City terminal at Moorgate, as well as the possibilities of through services to the Midland and Great Northern companies. There was direct passenger access to the Low Level station while this remained open. The revival of what is now termed Thameslink started with a limited service on the reinstated railway, but further expansion needed Holborn Viaduct station closed. Its last train departed on 26 January 1990 and a new lower level route to Farringdon was built. Today's railway runs beneath Ludgate Hill (road), resulting in the railway bridge that obstructed the view of St Paul's Cathedral being removed. This was the prelude to the creation of the present Thameslink service and the building of City Thameslink station. That was opened on 29 May 1990 as St Paul's Thameslink, but was renamed the following year. *Ref. AAJ 5687.*

Closures of electrified lines have been quite rare, but such was the fate of the 3¾ mile Crystal Palace High Level branch. The last day of service was 18 September 1954, and included also the stations of Upper Sydenham, Lordship Lane and Honor Oak before reaching the junctions at Nunhead station. This London, Chatham & Dover Railway branch had a chequered history. It was opened in 1865, 11 years after the Brighton Company's Crystal Palace Low Level station. According to the Southern Railway, they were nearly ¾ mile apart. The High Level station was of grand construction as this photograph taken on the final day of operation shows. This was the view looking south from within the train shed and it can be seen by the wagons present that some form of clearance work was already in progress. The station had three island platforms but only four tracks, so passengers were able to join and alight from either side of the train in the two central roads. As can be seen, the tracks converged at the far end of the building, to reach a turntable for locomotives. Trains reached the High Level station by way of Paxton Tunnel, with the station itself on an excavated site below the level of the nearby Crystal Palace Parade (A212). To reach the Palace itself (built for the Great Exhibition in Hyde Park 1851, then moved to this site in 1854 and destroyed by fire 1936), rail passengers would have to climb up to and then cross this road. The result was the building of a subway crafted in best Victorian style – but only for the use of First Class rail passengers. The loss of the Palace together with wartime damage to the railway sealed the fate of the branch from Nunhead. The last Southern Railway timetable of 1947 shows off peak services terminating at Nunhead, with other trains running through to Blackfriars or, occasionally, Holborn Viaduct. By then, all trains were Third Class only. Closure was the perhaps inevitable outcome. *Ref. AAJ 1675.*

Opposite top: Charing Cross, the West End terminus of the South Eastern Railway, could hardly be better situated for the centre of London. There was however a price to pay in terms of the number of platforms, six, and the length constraints given their closeness to the nearside bank of the Thames. In this picture of 30 May 1958, the 12:20 to Hastings behind an unidentified 'Schools' class 4-4-0 is preparing to leave from Platform 5. The staff member with his head behind the tender is checking on the progress being made on coupling up. All 40 of the 'Schools' class were allocated to sheds serving Kent, either the main or sub-sheds of '73' Stewarts Lane or '74' Ashford. Much appreciated because of their fleetness of foot, these locomotives designed by Maunsell first appeared in 1930, with modifications carried out on some of them by Bulleid in 1938. Not the least of their attributes

was their weight; 67 tons for a locomotive is certainly on the lighter side and Hungerford Bridge (the railway bridge over the river) did have its limitations. But the Kent Coast electrification was coming and that would see the end of steam locomotive working into Charing Cross. By now, the four running lines from Waterloo East had become, from the eastern side, down slow, up slow, down fast and up fast. At Charing Cross, these fed into and out of platforms 1 to 3 and 4 to 6 respectively. The fast line platforms are that much longer and consequently take up that much more room on the tightly constrained concourse. *Ref. AAJ 3467.*

Opposite bottom: Hungerford Bridge over the Thames is immediately outside Charing Cross station; it sees 2-EPB No. 5731 (Class 416/2) approaching the terminus on 9 July 1955 at the head of a train (headcode 12) from Orpington. The operational difficulties of working in such a confined area with a heavy peak traffic requirement will be appreciated. These trains were built as two-car units at Eastleigh works from 1954 to 1958, as part of the scheme to make South Eastern services up to 10 rather than eight cars. They featured 186 Second Class seats in a 3+2 layout. A fleet of 80 such units ensued. These were described as a typical British Railways design for the period, being a standard suburban layout with open saloons, no gangways between vehicles and no toilets. They were functional, bordering on the austere, with naked light bulbs for illumination after dark. They were equipped with two English Electric 250hp traction motors. A further 15 similar, but not identical, units followed for the South Tyneside electric services. When this line was dieselised in 1963, these units were absorbed into the Southern Region fleet, with the single First Class compartment they had been provided with in the north downgraded to Second Class. The destination blinds were of course removed. *Ref. AAJ 1980.*

Above: Hungerford Bridge joins Charing Cross station north of the Thames with Waterloo East on the south side. This view of 25 September 1969 is taken from the north bank and up stream of the bridge. The bridge is 441 yards long, a fraction more than a quarter of a mile. Above it can be seen part of the station signal box, with its commanding view of proceedings. Control was later moved to the London Bridge Area Signalling Centre, which opened in 1974. Emphasising that this is not a modern picture, the placard for the now long departed Evening News reads: 'My life as a Skinhead, Special Report'. It is also not the most beautiful of bridges with the railway bridges across the Thames coming in for serious criticism in the press in the 1930s. "They were ugly and should be demolished, and so should many of the viaducts on the south bank which lead to them. Charing Cross rail services could be terminated at Waterloo East, and so on. Passenger distribution from London Bridge could be by a series of new underground rail tunnels." There seems to have been little or even no consideration of the needs of the rail passenger for schemes which, for the most part, were impractical and were certainly unfunded. It was reported that Sir Herbert Walker told his disconsolate senior Southern officers not to worry: "Charing Cross bridge will still be there long after I have gone". Walker died in 1949 whilst the bridge remains and has since been enhanced by new pedestrian walkways across the river on both sides. *Ref. AAJ 6402.*

Opposite top: Cannon Street terminus in the City of London sees an unkempt Bulleid West Country class 4-6-2 Pacific No. 34037 *Clovelly* getting ready to leave with the last regular steam service to Ramsgate on Saturday 13 June 1959. By now, Phase 1 of the Kent Coast Electrification was well advanced and the 4-CEPs, 4-BEPs and 2-HAPs would be in charge of nearly all the principal workings from the following Monday. Taken from an electric train entering the station, an electric unit with headcode 41 will soon be departing for Dartford via Sidcup. Notable is the complexity of trackwork, designed to facilitate entry to and exit from any platform and any of the tracks to London Bridge. The other two tracks across the Thames are more restricted and lead in the other direction towards Charing Cross. Originally

provided so that Charing Cross trains could call at Cannon Street, reverse, and continue to Charing Cross, this time consuming manoeuvre was later discontinued and its use today is mainly in connection with engineering works. The red brick tower is one of a pair which used to support the station's overall roof. The roof received wartime damage and was eventually removed in 1958. The towers were Grade II listed in 1972. *Ref. AAJ 3999.*

Opposite bottom: This view of London Bridge approaches from a South Eastern train shows the two separate stations of the South Eastern & Chatham Railway, and the London, Brighton & South Coast. It also shows just how many tracks there are. On the Brighton side, Standard Class 4 2-6-4T No. 80019 gives the impression that it is about to back out of the siding in which it is held, but close inspection reveals that it is hemmed in by the coaching stock of the arrived train. Perhaps the latter is still moving; if it isn't, the tank locomotive is going to be staying there until some other means of release is found. The date is 7 June 1958. The length of platforms and hence their ability to accommodate trains of a given length, particularly at terminals as here, can be as important as their number. London Bridge used to suffer from short platforms on the most southerly side. However, the withdrawal of the short trains running via Denmark Hill to Victoria eased matters, and following the rebuilding that has taken place in recent years, the Brighton line platforms have been reduced from nine to six, and those on the South Eastern side have increased from six (and one through line with no platform) to nine. Importantly, all platforms can now accommodate 12-car trains. The new layout has helped to make Thameslink possible. *Ref. AAJ 3486.*

Above: This is the scene of a tragic accident which took place here near St John's station, Lewisham, in the early evening of 4 December 1957. The 17:18 Charing Cross to Hayes, a multiple unit made up to 10 cars and carrying around 700 passengers was stopped at a signal on the track immediately to the right of the bridge support column, with its brakes on. It was struck from behind at around 30 mph by the 16:56 Charing Cross to Ramsgate, with 11 coaches, hauled by Battle of Britain class steam locomotive No. 34066 *Spitfire*. In the words of the Accident Report: "The rear of the engine tender and the front of the leading coach were crushed together and then thrown to the left by the sudden stoppage, most unfortunately striking and dislodging a steel middle column supporting two of the four heavy girders of the bridge …' (which collapsed). This incident took place in dense fog, after the driver of the steam locomotive had passed colour light signals showing, successively, double yellow, single yellow and red aspects. The death toll was 90 and 173 people were injured. A worse outcome was narrowly averted when a third train, which was about to pass over the bridge, stopped just in time." The Inspecting Officer's report commented that had the Automatic Warning System been installed (giving the driver audible and visual indications of the signals, with the back up of brake application if not acknowledged), this accident might well have been averted. For their part, the British Transport Commission said that its installation would be progressed as fast as possible. This view of part of the site was taken on 16 July 1955, more than a year before this incident happened. *Ref. AAJ 2014.*

Top: Elmers End was a four platform station, seen here on 30 June 1973 from a train arriving from Hayes. On the left is a train in the platform used by the shuttle services to Addiscombe and to Sanderstead. The platform is occupied by a 2-EPB set for Woodside (served by both sets of trains) and then to the Addiscombe terminus. In those days, the shuttle to Addiscombe ran at half hourly intervals all day and every day, with Monday to Friday peak augmentation. A few of these ran through to Charing Cross or Cannon Street. All services from Hayes ran through to one of those London termini but to Charing Cross only outside the peak. These too had some peak additions. The Sanderstead line was less well served, with a maximum of nine trains in the peak direction (fewer in reverse), mornings and evenings, Mondays to Fridays. Several of these originated only from Selsdon, but some of these too were sent on to Charing Cross or Cannon Street. There was no service at all at other times or on other days. The last train to Addiscombe ran on 31 May 1997. That line from the junction south of Woodside was closed permanently, but much of the remainder became part of Croydon Tramlink from May 2000. The same bay platform at Elmers End, with a passing loop south of the platform, is still used for Tramlink services. *Ref. AAJ 7145.*

Bottom: This is Selsdon station from the carriage window as the train from Elmers End to Sanderstead passes over the junction beyond the platforms on 28 April 1962. This line was electrified by the Southern Railway on 30 September 1935. The line on the left climbed up from the Brighton main line, carrying trains from East Croydon and destined for Oxted and stations south. Note that it was not electrified; that was to come later, to East Grinstead but not to Uckfield. The Selsdon platforms serving that line were closed on 14 June 1959, by which time the service was of a token nature only. The buildings were demolished in 1963. In any event, Sanderstead station was only 50 chains beyond Selsdon, with South Croydon station 30 chains the other way, so its loss would hardly have been catastrophic. The line from Elmers End to Sanderstead arose from competition between the railway companies – the South Eastern and the London, Brighton and South Coast. It was not a success, partly because of the proximity of stations on other lines, which may have offered a greater frequency of services, but also because it only skirted around the edge of Croydon. The service was slated for closure before the Beeching Reshaping Report of 1963 was published. Closure would have taken place on 4 March 1963, but the proposal was refused by the Minister. Twenty years on, another attempt was successful, and the last trains ran on Friday 13 May 1983. *Ref. AAJ 4583.*

"It has always been the intention that, as soon as circumstances permit, all the main routes of the Southern Region east of a line drawn from Reading to Portsmouth should be electrified. This will extend to the coast the electrified zone which now terminates at Gillingham, Maidstone and (via Ashford) to Hastings. In conjunction with the diesel services to be introduced, this will effect the elimination of steam traction from all the lines of the Southern Region in the area mentioned". From the British Transport Commission plan for the Modernisation and Re-equipment of British Railways, December 1954. The poster, which gave details of the main works to be undertaken, was photographed at Blackheath station on 20 December 1958. In the event, Hastings had to wait rather longer for an electrified service south of Tonbridge due mainly to the severely restricted clearances in the double track tunnels on this route, and the line thence to Ashford is still diesel worked. The line to Bexhill West was closed on 15 June 1964, while regular services on the branches to Dover Marine and Folkestone Harbour ceased in 1994 and 2000 respectively. This followed the opening of the Channel Tunnel and the commissioning of High Speed 1.
Ref. AAJ 3775.

YOUR TRAIN
may be late and you want to know why

The railway between London and the Kent Coast is being rebuilt to take electric trains.

Massive engineering works are taking place which cause trains to be run at reduced speeds.

This means delay to trains on the lines affected by the engineering works, and reacts on other trains using the London terminal stations, especially during peak hour travel.

Everything possible is being done to keep these delays to a minimum.

This is what is happening and where:

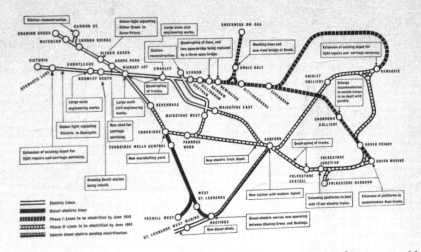

The inconvenience caused to passengers is regretted

SOUTH EASTERN DIVISION · Modernisation

85

Above: Major works in connection with the Kent Coast electrification included quadrupling the double track between Chislehurst and Swanley Junction. This is the section to St Mary Cray, seen here on 12 July 1958. Of note is the amount of work in progress while the line was clearly still open for traffic at, presumably, much reduced speeds. Cutting enlargement is in full swing, which requires a major effort associated with spoil removal. One of the major problems was that the railways in this area were built, competitively, by the South Eastern Railway and then the interloper, the London Chatham & Dover Railway. The Chislehurst flyovers were where the two crossed, with the Chatham at the lower level and the South Eastern above. A united system would provide new connections and much more flexibility in operations. The challenge was to provide for effective movement between the lines of each railway, both of which would end up as four track lines. That included the connection of the pairs of fast lines and the pairs of slow lines with the minimum of conflicting moves. The whole was carried out in two parts. Phase 1 covered the Chatham lines in North Kent via Faversham to Ramsgate and to Dover. Phase 2 concentrated on the South Eastern lines via Ashford. *Ref. AAJ 3558.*

Opposite top: This is Eltham Well Hall station and signal box on the Bexleyheath line on an uneventful 15 August 1969, looking towards London and before the Dartford resignalling. Here, on 11 June 1972, a returning excursion for railway employees and their families from Margate back to Kentish Town was derailed. The Class 47 locomotive No. D1630 was hauling 10 Mk1 coaches and virtually the whole train left the track on the severe curve beyond the station, seen here. Six people were killed, including the driver, and 126 were injured. The cause was attributed to the driver not reducing speed, estimated at 65mph, on reaching the curve. This had a permanent speed restriction of 20mph. It emerged at the inquiry by the Railway Inspectorate that the excessive consumption of alcohol by the driver was the major factor in what happened. The driver had booked on duty by telephone, as he was permitted to do, but this also meant that the alcohol in his breath was unlikely to be detected. The Inspecting Officer recommended that the arrangements for booking on remotely needed reconsideration. *Ref. AAJ 6382.*

Bottom; The original Greenwich station, opened in 1838, was west of the present site; it was replaced on a new site on 12 April 1840. The present grand station building dates from 1878. Seen here on 15 February 1964, it was built by the South Eastern Railway. It is situated on the south side of the double track electrified line. As can be seen, there is a substantial forecourt, in use for car parking. Many railways south of the Thames were built on a succession of brick viaducts, and this one was no exception. There were two principal reasons; first, much of the land was already built up, and a high level line would minimise the amount of property demolition and land take. Of at least equal importance, the Admiralty wanted sufficient clearance for its vessels to pass underneath the bridges, on the assumption that these lines would, at some stage, be crossing the Thames. The land was higher on the north side, so this would cause few difficulties there. Of more recent construction is the Docklands Light Railway extension to Lewisham. This opened on 20 November 1999. The DLR passes under the National Rail lines as it rises in tunnel from beneath the Thames and Cutty Sark station. It then reaches the surface at Greenwich station, where it occupies Platforms 3 and 4. It continues south, also initially on viaduct, to Lewisham.
Ref. AAJ 5093.

The South Eastern station of Abbey Wood, seen here looking west towards Plumstead on a dull 15 August 1969, has changed out of all recognition. The two North Kent line side platforms are now two islands, serving a total of four tracks. Those on the north side (to the right) are reserved for Crossrail (Elizabeth line) terminating trains, the others for the existing South Eastern services to London Bridge and Cannon Street. The whole station has been comprehensively rebuilt and unsurprisingly the semaphore signalling no longer exists. The level crossing has been replaced by a high level road overbridge, a little further to the east. In the distance, on the right, are now the Plumstead infrastructure maintenance depot and some stabling sidings for Crossrail. Situated to the north and a mile or so distant is the housing area of Thamesmead. This extensive development on the south bank of the Thames dates from the late 1960s and consists mainly of social housing. Abbey Wood is the nearest rail station and is linked to Thamesmead by a number of bus services. An extension of the Docklands Light Railway from Gallions Reach to Thamesmead, which involves a new Thames crossing, is under consideration. Further eastwards extension of Crossrail might come about in future, perhaps even as far as Ebbsfleet in Kent. This would result in extensive interaction with South Eastern services, particularly around Dartford. *Ref. AAJ 6376.*

London Underground Sub-Surface Lines

"Closure of South Acton Underground station. London Transport announces that the branch line between South Acton and Acton Town will be closed after Saturday February 28. Buses on route 55 provide a service between Acton Town and the South Acton area." Such was the notice displayed at both stations. The single car train of G stock is arriving at South Acton on 21 February 1959, one week before final closure. Would be patronage for the return journey appears to be sparse. The short 56 chains (0.7 miles) branch journey took two minutes; if the driver put the kettle in the staff room on before leaving Acton Town, it would be boiling by the time he got back. The service was first operated on 13 June 1905; what was originally double track and connected physically to the adjacent North London Line at South Acton was reduced to single track on 14 February 1932. The two G stock cars of 1923 vintage, one of which is seen here, were numbered 4167 and 4176. That provided one to operate the shuttle service and one spare. They took over after being converted to double ended and driver only operated single cars in 1939. This work included the fitting of enhanced braking systems on this short and heavily curved and graded line. Something in the order of eight to 10 trains per hour was provided. At Acton Town in the rebuilt station the service used Platform 5, which is still there albeit without track and hidden behind hoardings. At South Acton the station platform was a little higher than those of the North London line built a quarter of a century earlier. Of these no trace remains, which is also generally true of the branch as a whole.
Ref. AAJ 3801.

Opposite top: The Piccadilly line, in tunnel, is directly below the District line, itself on the surface at Earl's Court station. The Piccadilly then rises to the surface to the west of and beyond the next District line station of West Kensington, where it takes up the centre position between the District tracks. This results in a two island platform station at Barons Court, Piccadilly in the middle, District on the outside. A westbound Piccadilly train is seen here on 6 April 1957, coming to the surface beneath the then signal box. This looks to be a somewhat uncomfortable position for the signalling staff, with access not the easiest. It has since been decommissioned and demolished. Of note are the four tracks provided for the District for a short distance of around 300 metres, as these became two tracks again before reaching Barons Court. To judge by the apparent wear on them, usage was by this time modest. They have since been lifted. Behind the camera and to the south of the West Kensington station platforms, there were junctions leading to a goods yard (1878-1965). This was an outpost of the Midland Railway, which worked goods trains from Cricklewood, via the Dudding Hill line, then the curve between Bollo Lane and Acton Lane junctions, and via Turnham Green to West Kensington. The two loops served as locations where goods trains could be held clear of the principal running lines as necessary. *Ref. AAJ 2805.*

Opposite bottom: A train of Q stock from Kensington Olympia descends the gradient to join the District main line at West Kensington East Junction, en route for Earl's Court and (possibly) High Street Kensington. This was the favoured destination for Olympia shuttles, as it kept them out of the way of other services as much as possible. The District line now only serves Olympia when the situation so demands. It is 30 March 1957. Part of a battery electric locomotive may be seen at a higher level on the left in the Underground's Lillie Bridge depot. On the right is the West London line, which provides an important link between Willesden and Clapham Junctions. Today the main passenger traffic on it is provided by London Overground; in the days depicted, there were two trains daily in each direction. Other users have been InterCity, when through services were operated to and from Brighton, to Kensington Olympia from the north during the Paddington modernisation, Motor-rail services, for which Kensington Olympia was a London terminus, and sundry other cross-London passenger operations. These included, for instance, summer holiday traffic between the Midlands and South Coast resorts. Or, of course, freight. This amounts to the only feasible route between lines north and south of the Thames, and the series of junctions at each end reflect this. *Ref. AAJ 2792.*

Above: Fulham Broadway station sees one of the long time District line stalwarts of the R stock approaching, with a train for Wimbledon on 1 July 1967. The station opened on 1 March 1880 under the name of Walham Green; it took its present name on 2 March 1952. Much of the view in this picture is now hidden with the construction of a shopping centre over the station, resulting in a lowering of the roof above the platforms and the track immediately beyond. A limited section of the original roof remains. The rebuilding produced a new station entrance, leading to a footbridge serving both platforms; the bridge from which the photograph is taken was original. This led from the imposing District Railway façade on the station entrance in Fulham Road and afforded access via a sloping arcade-style passageway, having the ticket windows built into the design. This part is no longer available to be seen by the pubic, although it is understood to have been preserved. *Ref. AAJ 5979.*

Above: The Cromwell Curve area is east of Earl's Court and consists of the triangle of lines formed, left, of the District main line with an R stock train approaching, right, the Circle line route from Gloucester Road to High Street Kensington and, mostly out of sight, the line from Earl's Court to High Street Kensington used by the District's Wimbledon to Edgware Road services. It is 28 April 1956. The lights display on the front of the R stock train is the code for an eastbound train to Upminster. Such coding was discontinued after the R stock deliveries were complete, to be replaced by marker lights on the cab ends. This whole area was then largely in the open air and full of sidings. Today, most of this has been covered over and developed; only three sidings remain and are adjacent to the far tracks in this picture. A major requirement was space in which to build the West London Air Terminal. Various rail schemes to link central London with Heathrow had met with objections on the grounds of cost or practicality. What turned out to be only an interim solution was the in town air terminal, linked with the airport using a special build of double deck Routemaster buses towing luggage trailers. The extension of the Piccadilly line to what was then called Heathrow Central did not come about until 1977. *Ref. AAJ 2326.*

Opposite top: On 19 July 1958, an eastbound District line train of R stock in train red is seen arriving at a gas-lit Upton Park station, destination Upminster. The silver paint or aluminium finish which would eventually distinguish the R stock fleet had yet to be applied. The extension of District line services over or alongside the tracks of the London, Tilbury & Southend Railway started in 1902 as far as Barking, to be joined by the Metropolitan (now Hammersmith & City) in 1936. The western end of this section was at the former Campbell Road Junction, to the west of what is now Bromley-by-Bow station. Limited District services continued east of Barking to Upminster, but this did not become a permanent arrangement until 1932 in conjunction with four tracking. This was one of those complex cases of who owned what, whose trains had priority, and who should pay for what? There were platforms generally on both sets of lines as can be seen here, although later on only those at Barking and Upminster were in regular use for London, Tilbury & Southend trains. Elsewhere, some of the disused platforms were retained in usable condition. What amounted to the total operational separation of London Transport and British Rail tracks allowed responsibilities to be divided accordingly. New platforms were provided on the Tilbury line tracks at West Ham on 30 May 1999, offering additional interchange with the Jubilee line, London Overground and the Docklands Light Railway. *Ref. AAJ 3566.*

Bottom: This is the view from the south of Surrey Docks (now Surrey Quays) station towards the platforms which can just be seen. It is 2 June 1971 and two trains of Q23 stock are about to pass. They are part of a fleet of seven such four car trains which provided the East London line services from 1963 to 1971, when they were replaced with CO/CP stock. They were based at the line depot at New Cross. Operation of the East London has always had to take into account the two southern branches which divide at Canal Junction, 55 chains beyond Surrey Quays. The route to New Cross

connects only to South Eastern services on National Rail, as before. That to New Cross Gate reaches the Brighton line. Traditionally, the service was split equally to each branch, but now rather than just New Cross Gate, today's services use a grade separated junction to reach that station and continue on National Rail lines to either Crystal Place or West Croydon. Yet more services run from the new Silwood Junction, only 20 chains south of Surrey Quays, and make use of a long abandoned formation to join the Brighton lines at Old Kent Road Junction. They then run via Peckham Rye and Denmark Hill to Clapham Junction, terminating there. All services using the East London line are operated by London Overground, as successors to London Underground, with Class 378/1 dc third rail stock. *Ref. AAJ 6713.*

Left: The East London line of London Transport as it was on 19 February 1955 when this photograph was taken was a more or less self-contained bit of railway. It ran between what was left of Shoreditch station (seen here) to Surrey Docks (the present Surrey Quays) and then to either New Cross or to New Cross Gate. A connection to the Great Eastern line, facing towards Liverpool Street was still available (the track at the disused platform on the left), but usage by this stage was minimal. The line was then operated by F stock trains, seen here ready to depart and with an oil tail lamp on the back. These trains had three pairs of double doors on the side of each vehicle, which made them very good at shifting large crowds as this kept the station stop times down. Quite how often such tasks might have presented themselves on the East London line is a matter for conjecture. The same crowd shifting ability could be attributed to their 1960s successors, the C stock. The F stock was instantly recognisable from the elliptical windows on the ends of the driver's cabs. They ran on the East London line until 7 September 1963. *Ref. AAJ 1810.*

Opposite bottom: That the first stage of the Metropolitan Railway opened between Farringdon and Paddington in 1863 is well known; much less well known is that a westward extension to a station in Hammersmith followed only a year later. This was the result of collaboration with the Great Western Railway; among that company's contributions was building the Hammersmith depot, seen here on 17 October 1970, to be used and maintained by the Metropolitan. Large orders for new rolling stock for what is now the Hammersmith & City line, but also sections of the District and Metropolitan lines, were placed by London Transport in the 1930s. There were essentially two separate builds of O and P stock, although they did look similar to the uninitiated. The O stock was for the Hammersmith & City, with delivery from 1937 onwards. Later conversions produced a combined fleet of CO/CP stock, seen here. A notable feature of the design was the flared skirt, aimed at preventing passengers from jumping onto what would otherwise be running boards, making their way in as the train began to depart. This was indeed possible with passenger operated sliding doors, but not with the new-fangled air-operated ones. In this picture, close inspection shows that roads 1 and 2 have a CO Driving Motor Car, while roads 3 and 4 have a CP vehicle leading. A different note is struck on road 5, with one of the then very new C69 stock trains labelled 'Special'. The O and P rolling stock as originally delivered had a number of differences. Was the Guard to ride in the front of the last saloon, or in the rear driver's cab? The latter was a problem if platform lengths were on the short side. Was the mix of motored cars and trailers right? How reliable were the various types of technical equipment? How do you ensure the right mix of vehicles on a train if you want to alter the train lengths? Modifications over the years produced an acceptable balance, and the CO/CP stock trains last ran in 1981. *Ref. AAJ 6629.*

Above: Neasden Depot still gives the strong impression that this is the depot of the important Metropolitan Railway. This scene is dated 20 July 1957. On the left is a train of the Metropolitan's T stock, built for services to Watford, opened as an electrified railway in 1925. By contrast, services on the main line to Amersham, Chesham and Aylesbury were coaches hauled by electric locomotives as far as the fourth rail would take them. In the 1950s, this was Rickmansworth and British Railways steam locomotives then deputised. All the T stock trains were compartment stock, finished externally in varnished teak. A total of 157 cars were built, consisting of 60 Driving Motors with six third class compartments, a luggage space and a cab, 32 Driving Trailers with eight third class compartments and a cab, 34 Trailers with seven first class compartments, and 31 Trailers with nine third class compartments. They were built in batches, from 1920 to 1933, the oldest ones including vehicles from converted steam stock. They were far from a uniform design and after some fleet rationalisation were made up latterly into ten six-car trains and nine eight-car trains, one of each length being a spare. All would have had two Driving Motors and four or six intermediate trailers. The last time a T stock train ran in passenger service was on 5 October 1962. Elsewhere can be seen two Electric Sleet Locomotives, a CO/CP stock train and an F stock train. *Ref. AAJ 3098.*

Opposite top: London Transport's acquisition from British Railways of a fleet of former Great Western 0-6-0 Pannier tank engines between 1956 and 1963 did seem a little eccentric. Why was a virtually all-electric railway wanting to buy superannuated steam locomotives in an era when the modernisation of motive power was a primary aim? This is Pannier No. L91 at Neasden on 20 July 1957, formerly British Railways No. 5752. London Transport was to use this fleet on such freight operations that remained, engineering and ballast trains; they were never employed on ordinary passenger duties. Providing structural clearances were sufficient, they could be used extensively on the sub-surface system of the Underground, whether or not the traction current was switched on. Clearances were such that they could not operate on tube lines, which were the preserve of the battery locomotive fleet, while steam traction in tunnelled sections was not the best of ideas anyway. They were based at Neasden or Lillie Bridge; regular duties included taking waste material to the Croxley (Watford) tip. There was a maximum of 11 locomotives in the fleet at any one time (two were withdrawn while others were still being acquired). Last orders came on 6 June 1971, when No. L94 (BR No. 7752) hauled a permanent way special from Moorgate Widened Lines to Neasden Depot. They were replaced by three second hand diesel hydraulic locomotives, Nos. DL81, DL82 and DL83, built by Thomas Hill of Rotherham in 1967-68. A few of the Pannier tanks have survived into preservation, with some keeping their London Transport lined maroon livery. *Ref. AAJ 3088.*

Opposite top: The station at Rickmansworth was opened by the Metropolitan Railway on 1 September 1887. This was a terminus until 8 July 1889, when the line was extended to Chesham and subsequently to Amersham, and on 1 September 1892 to Aylesbury as part of the Metropolitan's push north. Services by the Great Central Railway here started on 15 March 1899. Railway electrification, after an uncertain start, reached Rickmansworth in 1925 as part of the joint scheme with what was by now the London & North Eastern Railway to construct a new line to Watford (Metropolitan). In this view of 27 September 1969 from the south can be seen the bay platform, put in by the Metropolitan, to enable them to provide a shuttle service to and from Watford (Metropolitan). Full electric services started on 2 November 1925 and from opening there were 30 trains a day each way on the shuttle using the north curve, but these proved to be uncompetitive with the bus services. They lasted no more than six months after the Metropolitan became part of the London Passenger Transport Board on 1 July 1933, finishing on 31 December of that year. Since then there has been sporadic service provision, mainly for stock positioning purposes. Rickmansworth station became the changeover point from electric to steam traction on 5 January 1925, a situation which was to persist until 10 September 1961. This followed the four tracking of the line from Harrow-on-the-Hill to Watford South Junction and electrification to Amersham and Chesham, which formed part of the much deferred 1935/40 New Works Programme. But at least it did actually happen, eventually. *Ref. AAJ 6414.*

Above: The Metropolitan Railway also handled goods traffic, though latterly it was a matter for British Railways. On 1 November 1957, this scene to the south of Rickmansworth station shows a goods shed with evidence of use by steam engines from the smoke above the entrance, plus copious supplies of wooden bodied coal wagons as well as what became the ubiquitous 16-ton minerals. The Metropolitan electric Bo-Bo locomotive, No. 10 *W E Gladstone*, still bears its Aylesbury destination board. It will have been detached from the train which it had brought from Aldgate, Liverpool Street or Baker Street, to be replaced by a British Railways locomotive. It is ideally placed to await the next steam hauled up working from Aylesbury, so that it can be attached for the journey back to London. Electrification to Amersham and Chesham, but not beyond to Aylesbury, was still some years away. With it would come the cessation of London Transport activities over the 14 miles beyond Amersham, with all rail services there to be provided by British Railways from London Marylebone. Later proposals that Aylesbury should become a Crossrail destination came to nothing, but the proposed extension of services to Bletchley and Milton Keynes Central as part of East West Rail do seem to be a possibility. *Ref. AAJ 3215.*

London Underground
Tube Lines: Bakerloo

Above: The Bakerloo line arrived at Edgware Road in 1907, but the extension to Queen's Park and the junction there with the London & North Western Railway was not completed until 1915. That was long enough for the lifts which characterised the earlier stations built to the designs of Leslie Green to be replaced by escalators, with the resultant lowering of the height of the building's roof. Escalators could also be taken down to platform level, avoiding the intermediate landing where lifts deposited their passenger. They then had to walk the last steps down to the trains. This is Maida Vale station entrance on 12 August 1961, with retail outlets within the station of Finlays Tobacconists and Barry's, a ladies' hairdresser. A flower barrow is seen on the right, while a passer-by picks up a newspaper. The Keep Left road sign dates from an era before white arrows on blue backgrounds replaced written material. Inside the station at a high level above the stairs leading down to the ticket office are two striking mosaics of UNDERGROUND roundels in full colour. *Ref. AAJ 4500.*

Right: The Bakerloo line was equipped with trains of 1938 stock, as seen in this picture of 4 July 1953 at Queen's Park. This view is from the southbound platform 2; one train is in service, approaching from the tunnels which lead ultimately to Elephant & Castle, the other is stabled in what is known as South Shed. A good proportion of the Bakerloo service terminates here. These trains run via the North Shed before returning. Other trains continued on British Railways tracks to Harrow & Wealdstone or, less frequently as the years progressed, to Watford Junction. Once north of Queen's Park, they were interworking with the dc electric services of the London Midland Region from Euston, so a lesser frequency of Underground services was appropriate. An odd feature of the trains that continued was that they had to use road 21 in the North Shed to reach British Railways property; coming south, they had to use road 24. Thus only roads 22 and 23 were available for reversing trains at all times. This was (and is) not a problem as such, since a two platform reversing feature is not uncommon elsewhere, such as at Elephant. However, to have a covered shed over the ordinary running lines is decidedly unusual. *Ref. AAJ 1170.*

London Underground
Tube Lines: Central Line.

Opposite top: An eight-car train of London Underground 1962 stock forms a westbound West Ruislip train between North Acton and Hanger Lane Central line stations. It was photographed from a train on the Great Western line on 13 August 1966. The bridge over the Central line tracks in the background carries the eastbound Central line trains from Ealing Broadway to North Acton Junction and into that station. The 1962 stock trains for the Central line were very close relatives to the Piccadilly's 1959 stock. The original intention was to use the 1960 stock, of which Cravens built 12 Driving Motors, but it was decided that pre-production testing would take too long, 'so stick with the devil you know'. The four-car units were made up of 50ft long vehicles comprising Driving Motor, Non-Driving Motor, Trailer, Driving Motor, with two units making up a train. As all the traction and ancillary equipment was beneath floor level or possibly under the seats, these new trains were claimed to

offer a 15% increase in capacity over those they replaced. All principal services on the Central line were provided by the 1962 stock by the end of that year. They were replaced by the 1992 stock. A few of the 1962 units (in seven car formations) survived on the Northern line before that too received new stock. *Ref. AAJ 5698.*

Opposite bottom: Just beyond the Central line's North Acton station, the line splits into its original route to Ealing Broadway, left, and what became the 1947-48 addition to West Ruislip. On 24 August 1957, a train of pre-1938 stock from Ealing Broadway is approaching the junction and it will be noticed that the trailing points it is yet to reach are set for a train from West Ruislip. This avoids any intervention to change the points, as the train wheels and its weight are sufficient to push the points across. Such arrangements are only practicable when the points are always approached from the trailing end and speeds are relatively modest. If other traffic arrangements might apply from time to time, such as during engineering works, the points can be clipped (with a clamp) and scotched (with a piece of wood to prevent them from moving physically). After the burrowing junction, the West Ruislip route runs broadly parallel to the former Great Western route from Paddington to Birmingham via Old Oak Common and High Wycombe. Then it was a double track main line, controlled here by lower quadrant semaphore signals as can be seen. Although much used in its heyday, the electrification of the London & North Western route from Euston resulted in traffic by the GW to fall away; it was reduced to single track and has since been disconnected in the Old Oak area. *Ref. AAJ 3172.*

Above: While it is possible to reverse trains with the use only of a simple crossover, this does presume that undue delays will not occur to other trains, on either line, while the manoeuvre takes place. Among the limitations are the need to make sure all passengers have left the train at the last station at which the train calls, the need for and the time taken for the driver to change ends, and the time for the move as the train re-enters service in the opposite direction. One (or more) turnback sidings in between the running lines is much to be preferred from an operational point of view. Such an arrangement can be found at Marble Arch, Central line. This view was taken on 8 June 1963 and shows, left to right, the westbound track continuing towards Shepherd's Bush, the dead end reversing tunnel and, just visible on the right, the connection from the reversing tunnel to the eastbound track. The wish to not run trains the full length of the route is based on what are likely to be diminishing load levels at the outer ends of the line. The result should be a service where the combination of train frequency and train occupancy best suits the overall service offered to the public. But you still need the whole fleet of trains for the peak service and running some of them on short(er) workings off peak may only result in quite modest savings. Some traction current and a bit of wear and tear, but what else? *Ref. AAJ 4888.*

Above: Gants Hill was a new station on the Central line extension beyond Liverpool Street. It was opened on 14 December 1947. From a subsurface ticket hall below a large roundabout, with subway exits to the surface in many directions, a bank of three escalators descend to this low level concourse, 150ft long and 20ft high. The trains on the two tracks (westbound on the right and eastbound on the left in this picture) can be seen readily by those waiting, on the seats facing the trains should they so choose. The fluorescent lighting, unusual for the period, may be noted. It is 19 July 1958. This was part of the Central line pushing out from the surface station at Leytonstone to that at Newbury Park, constructed largely under Eastern Avenue. Other intermediate stations are Wanstead and Redbridge. Work began at Gants Hill in 1937 on the station designed by Charles Holden, the architect who was responsible for many of the Underground stations in the inter-war period. Construction ceased during World War II hostilities, but enough had been done to enable the running tunnels to be used for wartime production work.
Ref. AAJ 3574.

Opposite top: Old Street station was opened on 17 November 1901 by the City & South London Railway as part of their extension north to reach Angel in 1901 and Euston in 1907. Provision was made for higher level tunnels and platforms to accommodate the Northern City line, which was opened on 14 February 1904 between Moorgate and Finsbury Park. This is directly above what is now the Northern line over common sections. The Northern line was closed between 8 August 1922 and 20 April 1924 so that the tunnels could be enlarged from the very restrictive diameters used by the City & South London to what became the standard tube gauge. This was coupled with the rebuilding of the original station to the designs of Stanley Heaps of the Underground Electric Railways of London (UERL) and Charles Holden, consultant architect, in 1925. Escalators replaced lifts for platform access. The building, at the north east corner of the City Road and Old Street junction, is seen here as it was on 19 September 1965. A large scale road improvement took place here and the surface station building was demolished in 1968. A series of access subways was provided and these led to a below ground ticket hall and barriers. No surface buildings remain. The Northern City line was closed on 4 October 1975, with ownership transferred to British Rail. The Great Northern Electrics service between Moorgate and Welwyn Garden City or Hertford North was inaugurated in August 1976, using the new dual voltage Class 313 suburban units.
Ref. AAJ 5566.

London Underground
Tube Lines: Northern City

Below: This is the original entrance to Highbury & Islington station, as opened by the Great Northern & City Railway for its new line between Moorgate and Finsbury Park on 28 June 1904. It was closed as part of the reconstruction work undertaken in conjunction with the building of the Victoria line. The entrance to all lines of Underground, Overground and National Rail is now on the other side of the road.

In this view of 1 September 1968, the disused building is looking very sorry for itself; it was eventually cleaned up, many years later. There were discussions in 2017 as to whether it could be resuscitated to ease the congestion which is endemic in the present station. This might provide a more satisfactory means of accessing the deep level Victoria line and National Rail's Great Northern electrics, which have cross platform interchange between them. At surface level, London Overground trains approaching from the East London line terminate here; these are third rail dc only trains. The other two tracks host the Clapham Junction/ Richmond -Stratford services. These trains have dual voltage capability, but are otherwise similar units of Class 378. *Ref. AAJ 6136.*

Above: This is a general view looking south of the whole of the Northern City line's Drayton Park station and depot area. It was taken on 2 July 1960. As can be seen, the station platforms are tightly wedged in, while the depot, which has to accommodate all the line's stock, is not over-generously provided with space, either. A number of the pre-1938 stock trains are in evidence. At the higher level, on the left, is the line from Finsbury Park to the North London Line at Canonbury and on to Broad Street. A BRC&W Type 2 (Nos D5300-I9 is running round a train of British Railways built suburban non-gangwayed coaches. These 57ft vehicles had nine straight through compartments, with six-a-side seating, giving a remarkable 108 seats in total. For those unfortunate enough to have to stand, a major problem for anybody not tall enough to reach the luggage racks was the lack of anything to hang onto, other than the knees of seated passengers. Built from 1954 onwards, they were austere. Lit only by bulbs in the ceiling, a mirror was provided on one of the compartment walls. In the Brake Second vehicle a Ladies Only compartment with its green label was provided next to the Guard's accommodation. They and a selection of locomotive types were standard fare for the inner-suburban Great Northern services, meeting their end in 1976 with the Great Northern electrification to Moorgate. *Ref. AAJ 4364.*

London Underground Tube Lines: Northern

Opposite bottom: Drayton Park, its island platform and depot are the only part of the Northern City line to be above ground. The whole was opened on 14 February 1904. Photographed on 27 March 1954, a train of pre-1938 stock arrives with a service from Finsbury Park to Moorgate. The Metropolitan Railway style station name board (this company owned the railway before the formation of London Transport in 1933) will be noted. To the right of the train is the route to the surface and the Finsbury Park to Canonbury (and Broad Street) line, used for taking the rolling stock to Acton Works. It may be noted that fire buckets were still provided on the platform. The railway was built to something approaching full sized loading gauge, since it was hoped that the line would one day be extended northwards. Or perhaps that would be the prerogative of the Piccadilly line, which reached Finsbury Park two years later, in 1906. In the end, the Great Northern and its London & North Eastern Railways successor raised objections, and while the Piccadilly achieved its extension to Cockfosters in 1933, the Northern City line stayed as it was. The London Transport New Works Programme of 1935/40 would have changed all that, but war stopped play. It was not until 1976 that the line became part of British Rail and the London end of the Great Northern Suburban Electrification. The fourth rail became third rail and Drayton Park the changeover point from (or to) the 25kV ac overhead system. *Ref. AAJ 1387.*

Above: At East Finchley, the Northern line comes to the surface of the 17 mile 526 yard tunnel from Morden (measured via Bank) and for a time the longest railway tunnel in the world. On 23 March 1957 a 1938 stock train, stalwart of the Northern line for the best part of 40 years, is about to disappear into the southbound tunnel. On the right is the former British Railways line from Finsbury Park, which was to form part of the Northern Heights scheme, but now only gives access to Highgate depot. The lengthy bridge in the foreground is there to take the railway across the A1000 High Road East Finchley at an acute angle. A similar arrangement may be found on the northbound Underground track, the other side of the British Railways lines. Reported plans that involved the diversion of some trains from the south to terminate in the largely redundant centre platforms at East Finchley (immediately behind the camera), then returning to central London, would need all the pointwork to be between the bridge and the tunnel mouths. Although the regular passenger train service of British Railways to East Finchley ceased with the introduction of Northern line services in 1939/40, the connection continued to be used. Occasional passenger excursions were run by British Railways from High Barnet via the Widened Lines to south coast destinations, while there was continued use by freight trains. These were headed by the Class N2 0-6-2 tanks, or later by the D8200 diesels (Class 15) based at Finsbury Park, serving the long existing goods yards. The last of these was closed in 1964. The longest use was for the Northern City Line (Moorgate-Finsbury Park) trains en route to overhaul at Acton Works. This involved being hauled from their Drayton Park depot, via the Finsbury Park route to East Finchley, reverse, then to King's Cross on the Northern and using the link there to the Piccadilly, reverse, thence to Acton Town, reverse, and Acton Works. This operation ceased when the infrastructure was deemed unsafe for further use and another route via King's Cross main line had to be devised. *Ref. AAJ 2770.*

Right: Of the Great Northern branches from Finsbury Park, only the sections from East Finchley to Finchley Central and then to High Barnet or Mill Hill East carry passenger trains today. These are part of London Undergrounds's Northern line. Seen here on 5 May 1956 is Finchley Central from a Locomotive Club of Great Britain society special leaving Mill Hill East branch platform. By now, much of the other sections of the route were there only because of their continuing use by goods traffic. Minimal

alterations were made to this station following the transfer of line ownership to London Transport, whose operations began in 1940/1. Electrification and resignalling, yes, but changes to Finchley Central saw little more than the lowering of platforms to match tube train height, in this case for 1938 stock. Earlier intentions to create a two-island, four platform station fell by the wayside due to the war, these were never subsequently revived. The station was however renamed Finchley Church End. *Ref. AAJ 2354.*

London Underground
Tube Lines: Piccadilly

Opposite bottom: There was one tunnel on the Northern line extension to Bushey Heath, at Elstree South. This is the southern portal, as seen on 8 May 1965. Only a few yards had been constructed before work ceased in 1939, never to be resumed. The spoil which largely fills the cutting leading to its entrance came from the proposed Aldenham Northern line depot site. As it turned out, this became a factory for wartime production and in the post war years was reinvented as London Transport's bus overhaul works. Those works were closed in November 1986 and sold; a decade later the building was demolished. The tunnels, seen here with construction vehicles above them, were to disappear altogether under the M1 motorway. That section of the motorway, south of Junction 4, was opened in 1967. *Ref. AAJ 5450.*

Above: Aldwych station should perhaps never have been built. The only operational platform is seen here on 10 March 1956, with the shuttle service carrying passengers over the 720 metre line to Holborn. Today's Piccadilly line, of which the branch was a part, was conceived as two separate undertakings. These were the Great Northern & Strand, and the Brompton & Piccadilly. But neither could find finance, and it was left to the American financier Charles Tyson Yerkes to acquire them both. Together with the District Railway, which he already owned, a combined scheme of the Great Northern, Piccadilly and Brompton was devised. Construction went ahead and the 14.17km line from Finsbury Park to Hammersmith was opened on 15 December 1906. The building works did include the branch to Aldwych, which was opened a year later on 30 November 1907. However, it was now peripheral to the main Piccadilly line. The junction at Holborn faced Finsbury Park and attempts to run through services towards Hammersmith did not last long. So the short branch remained as a shuttle from Holborn, where it had its own platform, latterly confined to peak hour operation only. The end came on 30 September 1994, when it was decided that, coupled with low patronage levels, the cost of replacing the original passenger lifts at Aldwych could not be justified. *Ref. AAJ 2247.*

Above: Cockfosters depot is on the south side of the Piccadilly line between the terminus and Oakwood. The running lines are at a slightly higher level, as seen here on 7 May 1966 with a train of 1959 stock passing on a westbound working. 'Westbound' is London Underground speak encompassing the general direction of the line which is indeed basically east-west. However, at this point the train is heading only slightly south of due east. The 1959 stock was built by Metro-Cammell for the Piccadilly and in the event was followed by the very similar 1962 stock for the Central. Train lengths were seven cars on the Piccadilly, with each train consisting of two unequal length sets. These were made up of Driving Motor, Trailer, Non-Driving Motor, Driving Motor, plus Driving Motor, Trailer, Driving Motor. It was much simpler on the Central line, as each half train could be the same. All these trains drew heavily on their 1938 stock forebears. The main differences noticeable by passengers were fluorescent strip lighting replacing the traditional bulbs, rubber suspension (bounce … bounce … bounce) in lieu of the more gentle leaf springs, and the train red livery giving way to unpainted aluminium. This picture shows a most unusual installation, described to staff as a Snow Clearing Device, with the purpose of keeping train roofs clear. Only 3km from Cockfosters trains have to enter the 849m Southgate tunnel, complete with its station platforms, then another 2km in the open before reaching the tunnel beyond Arnos Grove. This latter continues to Barons Court. Passengers waiting on the platforms do not appreciate being showered with snow from arriving trains, and it is at best an operational hazard. The lack of conductor rails immediately under the device will be noted. *Ref. AAJ 5661.*

Opposite bottom: The Victoria line's only excursion above ground is at the Northumberland Park depot, situated on the eastern side of British Rail's Lea Valley line and a little to the south of the station of the same name. This view is dated 19 September 1965, when opening was still three years away and there was clearly a lot to do. Looking north from the public footbridge that helpfully crosses the site, the depot control tower is in the course of construction. Staff in here would control the movements of all trains within the depot premises, contacting the drivers by radio. An illuminated panel diagram would show the position of every train. Points would all be set by the control tower operator. The large vacant area to the right would form stabling roads under cover but also workshop roads and those with maintenance pits. The complete rolling stock fleet for the whole line requires considerable space in which to be housed. During the construction period, a connection with the Lea Valley line (left) allowed the delivery of materials to the site by rail, using the Underground's battery locomotives. *Ref. AAJ 5456.*

London Underground Tube Lines: Victoria

Right: What was to become London Underground's Victoria line appeared in essence, later refined, as Route C in the British Transport Commissions London Plan Working Party report of 1949. Then matters stood still, for many years. The critics claimed that it represented a waste of resources and that it wasn't really necessary. If it must be built, couldn't it be done cheaper? It got its enabling Act of Parliament, but that on its own was not enough. There was still the little matter of funding to be sorted out. The Victoria line finally got the go ahead from government in 1962. Would it not provide a stimulus to the economy by boosting employment? The original line with its Automatic Train Operation and Driver but no Guard, opened in three stages: Walthamstow Central to Highbury & Islington on 1 September 1968; Highbury & Islington to Warren Street on 1 December 1968; Warren Street to Victoria on 7 March 1969. The extension from Victoria to Brixton was added subsequently and was opened on 23 July 1971, with Pimlico station coming later on 14 September 1972. That was the only station which did not have interchange with other Underground or National Rail lines, though Blackhorse Road interchange with the Tottenham & Hampstead line was a little nominal in the early days. This poster was photographed on 1 March 1969 at what was then the Vauxhall working site, six days before V Day on 7 March. *Ref. AAJ 6212.*

V-DAY IS MARCH 7

From 15 00 March 7 the Victoria Line opens up the West End-Oxford Circus, Green Park, Victoria. And a quick direct service between King's Cross, Euston and Victoria.

London's pride

Above: Looking south from that same Northumberland Park footbridge a couple of years later on 26 August 1967, the prominent building is the carriage washing plant for trains entering the depot when coming off duty. This can be bypassed if necessary, but normal practice will see trains washed. Trains arrive on the nearside tracks, departing on the far side. These lead in the distance to a pair of tracks descending to Seven Sisters below ground station. Uniquely for the Victoria line, Seven Sisters has three platforms. Platform 3 is for trains bound for Walthamstow Central, No. 4 can be used for trains to Walthamstow, but also gives access to the depot. Platform 5 is for trains to Brixton, whether they come from the depot or Walthamstow. Platform 4 can also be used for staff shuttle trains to and from the depot, the further points of which are well over 2km distant. Platforms 1 and 2, it might be added, are up the stairs and used by London Overground services between Liverpool Street and Enfield Town or Cheshunt. With today's fleet of 43 Victoria line trains, the maximum of a 36 trains per hour service frequency (a train every 100 seconds) and 15 stations with two platforms each (one with three), there is little spare capacity for anything, anywhere. Not all trains are in use at any one time as they do need to be maintained as well. *Ref. AAJ 5987.*

Opposite; On 22 June 1968, a couple of months before the first section of the new Victoria line started operation between Walthamstow and Highbury & Islington, four trains (or maybe part trains) of 1967 stock are seen in Northumberland Park depot. They consist of Driving Motors Nos. 3008, 3024, 3015 and 3011. This was a brand new depot with brand new trains, all lined up but with nowhere to go. In reality, there was much to do. Completion of tunnelling, ventilation, drainage, tracklaying, fitting out of stations, depot provision, maintenance arrangements, and electrification are obvious requirements, but so too are signalling and communications, the control organisation, staff recruitment, staff training, and trial running. What might be the full implications of Automatic Train Operations? It wasn't just a case of could it be made to work? That was certainly a requirement, but it also needed to perform as well as anticipated, to do so reliably, and safely, with the results to the general satisfaction of both the travelling public and the operators. Each train consisted of two identical four car units; initially, there were 30½ of them. The fleet was increased to 39 when the Brixton extension was built, and traffic growth resulted in the conversion of some similar 1972 stock to enable 43 trains to be formed. The present 47 trains of 2009 stock now provide all services. *Ref. AAJ 6106.*

London Underground
Tube Lines: Waterloo & City

The Southern's Waterloo & City line is a very limited operation with just two stations (Waterloo and Bank) and a length of 1 mile 38 chains. Trains are of tube size. This is Waterloo on 7 March 1953, with one of the 1940 built cars (latterly Class 487) in view. Arriving trains run forward into the reversing siding (as here), before setting back into the near platform for the return working. The fleet consisted of 12 Driving Motor cars and 16 Trailers; with a Driving Motor at each end with up to three Trailers between them. Motor cars were double ended and could be run singly. The cars were a mere 49 ft long, with 40 seats in the Motors and 52 in the Trailers. With such a short journey many passengers elect to stand, even if seats are available. There were two double doors on each side of the trailers, one of which was replaced by a single door on the driving motors. In 1956 the journey time on this double track railway was advertised as taking five minutes, running from 06:45 to 22:00 but on weekdays only (meaning not Sundays). The then single fare was 4d (1.7p) and through bookings were available to Liverpool Street, Moorgate and Tower Hill (for Fenchurch Street). Dogs, Bicycles and Perambulators (unfolded) were not carried. If they had been, as with ordinary rail services, a charge would have been made. The Class 487s lasted for a remarkable 53 years, being retired in 1993. They were replaced by London Underground 1992 stock as used on the Central line, and third rail traction became fourth rail. The Waterloo & City line is now part of London Underground, and has been since 1 April 1994. *Ref. AAJ 5905.*